BLOOD WORK endorsements

"Christians tend to speak of the blood of Christ either flippantly or not at all. However, in *Blood Work*, Anthony Carter helps us see that neither of these options is appropriate. The blood of Christ is a central biblical theme that deserves to be pondered deeply. Carter forces us to consider Christ's atoning sacrifice and its many implications. In the end, we are left with a glorious, cross-centered, Christ-centered gospel that gets to the heart of our great need and God's great provision. We are indeed purchased, redeemed, brought near, cleansed, sanctified, and freed by the blood of Christ. In a day awash with self-help books, it is refreshing to be reminded that we indeed cannot help ourselves, but God, through the blood of Christ, has done more than help us; He has saved us. Thank God for the blood!"

—DR. VODDIE BAUCHAM JR.
Pastor of preaching, Grace Family Baptist Church, Spring, Texas
Author of *Family Shepherds*

"This book will leave you in awe of the benefits of trusting in the finished work of Jesus on the cross. It is unquestionably thorough, remarkably captivating, and surprisingly clear. You'll leave this book singing, 'Nothing but the blood of Jesus.'"

—BRYAN LORITTS
Lead pastor, Fellowship Memphis, Memphis, Tenn.
Author of *A Cross Shaped Gospel*

"Anthony Carter has brought to our senses what many Christians have taken for granted, the precious blood of Christ. His scholarship and passion are evident. We need this book."

—LECRAE MOORE
Christian hip-hop artist
Founder and president, ReachLife Ministries and Reach Records

"*Blood Work* is both theologically rich and devotional. Anthony Carter presents a refreshing pastoral reminder of what the believer has been given through the finished work of Christ Jesus. This is a must read for the new believer, as well as for those who are well into the spiritual journey."

—DR. ROBERT H. ORNER
Dean of students, Reformed Theological Seminary,
Orlando, Fla.

"Salvation is possible only because of the shed blood of Christ. Tony Carter helps us to better understand and appreciate the full significance of this great sacrifice. This book will set Christ's sacrifice before you and allow you to view it from angles you've not seen before and others you may have seen but not fully appreciated. This is a great compact book that goes deep on a subject we can't talk about enough and for which we will never be able to thank God enough."

—VERMON PIERRE
Lead pastor, Roosevelt Community Church,
Phoenix, Ariz.

"Blood. It is considered vile to discuss. We are tempted to mark from our manuscripts any talk of it before we approach the pulpit. We purpose ourselves to talk around it when 'reaching out' to unbelieving friends. Yet, it is the blood of Christ that cries out 'Adopted! Forgiven! Free! Empowered! Entrusted! Kept!' to our broken souls. With this work, Anthony Carter reminds us that, though we may attempt to camouflage its role in every aspect of life in Christ, the blood will never lose its power. If we try to diminish its power, we will certainly lose ours."

—LEONCE B. CRUMP II
Founding pastor, Renovation Church, Atlanta, Ga.

BLOOD WORK

HOW *the* BLOOD *of* CHRIST
ACCOMPLISHES OUR SALVATION

ANTHONY J. CARTER

IR *Reformation Trust*   A DIVISION OF LIGONIER MINISTRIES, ORLANDO, FL

Blood Work: How the Blood of Christ Accomplishes Our Salvation

© 2013 by Anthony J. Carter

Published by Reformation Trust
a division of Ligonier Ministries
421 Ligonier Court, Sanford, FL 32771
Ligonier.org   ReformationTrust.com

Printed in Ann Arbor, Michigan
Sheridan Books, Inc.
January 2013
First edition

Cover design: Dual Identity, Inc.
Interior design and typeset: Katherine Lloyd, The DESK

Unless otherwise indicated, all Scripture quotations are from *The Holy Bible, English Standard Version*®, copyright © 2001 by Crossway Bibles, a publishing ministry of Good News Publishers. Used by permission. All rights reserved.

Scripture quotations marked KJV are from *The Holy Bible, King James Version*.

Library of Congress Cataloging-in-Publication Data

Carter, Anthony J., 1967-
  Blood work : how the blood of Christ accomplishes our salvation / Anthony J. Carter.
    p. cm.
  Includes bibliographical references.
  ISBN 978-1-56769-314-0
  1. Jesus Christ—Blood. 2. Salvation—Christianity. I. Title.
  BT590.B5C38 2013
  232'.4—dc23

                                        2012034785

To Christina

Contents

Acknowledgments

Though an author is often alone in his writing, he knows he is never really alone. I could never have written this book without the love and support of many people, a few of whom I want to mention and thank.

To the elders of the East Point Church family: As pastor, I count it a joy to serve with you. Your faithful encouragements and support are not taken for granted. I thank God for such a loving, gracious, giving, and prayerful church family.

To Lee and Ruth Fowler: Thanks for your help. Ruth, you are the best part-time/full-time administrator/graphic designer/conference and scheduling coordinator/faithful servant of Christ a church could ever have. Lee, thanks for your eyes and ears on this project. More than a teacher and a deacon, you are a friend.

To Allan Bynoe: In our longtime friendship, you have been more to me than a brother. Thank you for taking the unpolished musings of a pastor who thinks he's a poet and turning them into a song our church family has used to worship and make much of Christ.

To Ligonier Ministries, Greg Bailey, and Reformation Trust Publishing: Thank you for all you do. I could not imagine my life without the influence and encouragements of R. C. Sproul and Ligonier Ministries. Greg, thanks for your enthusiasm for this project. I pray God rewards your labors with fruit now and in years to come.

To my wife, Adriane, and our children, Tony Jr., Rachel, Sarah, Siera, and Ana: Thank you for loving and serving me without hesitation or complaint during the completion of this book. May our love and lives together be an ongoing celebration of the precious blood of Christ shed for us.

A DONOR FOR CHRISTINA

We were used to seeing delivery trucks come to the house. Being lovers of books, we regularly (sometimes daily) received packages from UPS or FedEx. So, when the FedEx truck pulled into the driveway one day, it was nothing out of the ordinary. However, as the driver walked to the door, it became clear that something was different this time. Rather than a package, he carried a letter.

Instead of coming from some online bookstore or publishing company, the delivery was from an organization known as "Be the Match." I had never heard of Be the Match and could not but wonder why it needed to send a letter to me in an overnight express envelope. I opened the envelope, not knowing what to expect except the unexpected. As I read the letter, my expectations were met, and then some. The letter read something like this:

Dear Mr. Carter:

We are writing to inform you that you have been identified as a possible match as a donor for a bone-marrow transplant patient. It is urgent that you contact us so we can confirm whether you are a complete match.

I was bewildered. How could I be a match for anyone? I didn't recall donating blood or signing up for a bone-marrow registry. Besides, how does one get on such a registry? I know the Internet is capable of hijacking a lot of our personal information, but can it get our blood types as well?

As I pondered the possibilities, something came to me. The only event I could remotely connect to the moment had happened more than eighteen years before. Back then, I had participated in a blood drive organized to find a bone-marrow match for a dear friend of ours. Could this unexpected letter be the result of my donating blood eighteen years prior? Even if it was, how had Be the Match found me eighteen years, two states, and six addresses later?

The year was 1994. Robert and Winnie Benson were friends of ours. Robert served as the associate pastor of the church we attended. They were faithful servants of God and parents to four children—a son and three daughters. Their middle daughter's name was Christina. In 1992, she had been diagnosed with leukemia. Christina was 9 years old. The sickness was unexpected and obviously life-altering.

After several treatments of chemotherapy, a hopeful remission of nearly two years, and a lot of prayer, the doctors determined that Christina would need a bone-marrow transplant if she was to survive. Unfortunately, no one in her family was a match for her. Therefore, the circle of potential marrow donors needed to be enlarged.

The call went out for a blood drive to be held at the church in March 1994. The response was tremendous. Not only did the church members come out in great numbers, so did people who lived in the surrounding community, and many more who had heard of young Christina's sickness. I was one of hundreds who donated blood that day (and apparently became part of a registry of individuals desiring to offer blood to save another's life). The day was filled with hope and anticipation. There was excitement and fervent prayer. Surely, out of all those people, someone would be identified as a donor for Christina. Unfortunately, the excitement of that day was overshadowed by the sobering news we received in the coming weeks—no match had been found.

With no match and the cancer taking more and more of her strength, it was only a matter of time. Christians around the world offered prayers. Christina battled the illness bravely and with a joy that humbled all who knew her. Nevertheless, to our dismay, Christina died on April 26, 1997. A Spirit-filled warrior to the end, her smile and consistent faith testified to the grace and love of her Lord and Savior Jesus Christ. She was welcomed into the rapturous presence of Christ because His blood did what our blood could not do—save her. Christina was 12 years old.

As I read over the letter from Be the Match again, I was not sure what to do. Many questions came to mind: What is the process for such a thing? What will it require of me? Will it hurt?

Who would receive the transplant from me? I hesitated to do it. How many people receive these notices every day and never give them a second thought? Besides, who has time for a drawn-out process and possible hospitalization for a period of time? Excuses and reasons for not responding to this letter flooded my mind. If I never responded, who would know?

Then it occurred to me: What would Christina want me to do? If someone had been a match for Christina, what would I have wanted him to do? What if it was my wife, son, or daughter who stood in need? How would I feel about a potential donor who ignored a request to save my wife or daughter? The decision was made. I quickly called and made an appointment for blood to be drawn and tests to be conducted.

At the local clinic, I did not know what to expect. The attending nurse, upon seeing my paperwork and noticing that I was being tested for a possible bone-marrow transplant, was amazed. She informed me that the majority of people ignore notices like the one I had received; she rarely saw anyone follow through with a request. I was shocked. Surely, I thought, the opportunity to offer life-saving assistance to another is something many of us would welcome with enthusiasm. Sadly, this is not the case.

Unfortunately, after the blood was drawn and the tests were conducted, it was determined that I was not a match. Honestly, I was a little disappointed. The idea of saving someone's life had grown on me. Nevertheless, my name remains on the registry, and I could receive another overnight express envelope any day.

As I went through that dramatic ordeal, it was impressed upon me just how precious blood is. It literally is the difference between life and death. But even though my blood could potentially save the temporal life of one, how many more can be saved unto eternal life by the precious blood of Jesus? If I could give my blood and by doing so give life to another, how much more life can the blood of Jesus give? These thoughts led to the book you hold in your hands. Consider it a celebration of the life-giving, soul-blessing, power-enduing blood of Jesus.

This book is dedicated to Christina, because God used her to remind me that life is truly in the blood. Temporally, it is in the blood running through our veins. Eternally, it is in the sin-breaking, guilt-removing, incomparable, inestimably valuable blood of Jesus Christ.

It is my prayer that as you read, you will be encouraged to sing with new meaning:

> *O precious is the flow*
> *That makes us white as snow.*
> *No other fount I know.*
> *Nothing but the blood of Jesus.*[1]

One

OUR BLOODY RELIGION

There is a fountain filled with blood,
Drawn from Immanuel's veins;
And sinners, plunged beneath that flood,
Lose all their guilty stains.[2]
—WILLIAM COWPER

I t has been said that Christianity is a bloody religion. Critics usually make this accusation, pointing to the wars, inquisitions, trials, and executions carried out over the years in the name of Christianity. We must admit that blood has been wrongly shed in the name of so-called Christianity, but Christianity would be a bloody religion regardless. It is a bloody religion not because of the blood shed by people in wars and inquisitions, but because of the blood shed by Jesus Christ.

What is blood? Blood is the life-giving and life-maintaining fluid that circulates through the body's heart, arteries, veins, and capillaries. Here are some interesting and important facts about blood:

- The average person's blood is approximately 8 percent of his body weight.
- Healthy kidneys recycle four hundred gallons of blood every day.
- The average woman has about 4.5 liters of blood in her body. The average man has about 5.5.
- Because blood leaves an indelible stain, Native Americans used it for paint.
- During the early nineteenth century, it was believed that riding on a carousel would improve blood circulation.
- One out of every seven people entering the hospital needs blood.
- Someone needs blood every two seconds.
- One pint of blood can save three lives.

Here is an undeniable and important fact: *Blood gives and maintains lives.*

Christians should know this better than others. In the preface to the book *Precious Blood*, Richard Phillips writes, "At the very heart of our Christian faith is a precious red substance; the blood of our Lord Jesus Christ."[3] To read the Bible with any seriousness and sober discernment is to see the shedding of blood or the implications of it on practically every page. If the history of redemption is a story told in pictures, the blood of Christ is the paint with which that story is portrayed.

The history of Christianity is filled with blood. More than anything else, the Bible speaks of the blood of Christ accomplishing for us the grand benefits that belong to salvation: We have been purchased by His blood (Acts 20:28). We have propitiation by His blood (Rom. 3:25). We have been justified by His blood (Rom. 5:9). We have redemption through His blood (Eph. 1:7). We who were afar off have been brought near by His blood (Eph. 2:13). We have peace through His blood (Col. 1:20). Our consciences are cleansed by His blood (Heb. 9:14). We are sanctified through His blood (Heb. 13:12). We are elect in His blood (1 Peter 1:1–2). We are ransomed by His blood (1 Peter 1:18–19). We have been set free from sin by His blood (Rev. 1:5). These and many other benefits remind us that the blood of Christ is central to all we are as a redeemed people. Therefore, we will consider each of these benefits chapter by chapter.

In examining and explaining the meaning of the blood of Christ, the seventeenth-century Puritan Stephen Charnock wrote:

> By this is meant the last act in the tragedy of his life, his blood being the ransom of our souls, the price of our redemption, and the expiation of our sin. The shedding of his blood was the highest and most excellent part of his obedience (Phil. 2:8). His whole life was a continual suffering, but his death was the top and complement of

his obedience, for in that he manifested the greatest love
to God and the highest charity to man.[4]

The significance of the blood of Jesus also can be seen in
how frequently it is mentioned. In fact, "the 'blood' of Christ is
mentioned in the writings of the New Testament nearly three
times as often as 'the cross' of Christ and five times as frequently
as the 'death' of Christ."[5]

Therefore, it should not be surprising that as recipients of
God's gracious salvation through the person and work of Christ,
we preach, pray, and even sing of the wonderful power of His
blood, as the popular hymn by William Cowper demonstrates:

> *There is a fountain filled with blood,*
> *Drawn from Immanuel's veins;|*
> *And sinners, plunged beneath that flood,*
> *Lose all their guilty stains.*[6]

The Bible speaks of the blood of Christ as affecting and
impacting everything we do as a community of faith. In fact, not
only do we preach, pray, and sing the blood of Jesus, we even
participate in it.

When we come to the Lord's Table and receive Communion, the Bible reminds us, the cup we receive is the blood of
Christ. The language, in fact, is that of fellowship: "The cup of
blessing that we bless, is it not a *participation* in the blood of
Christ?" (1 Cor. 10:16, emphasis added). The word translated
as "participation" is the Greek word *koinonia*, which also means

"fellowship." It is a description of our communion with one another (Acts 2:42) and of our union with Christ (1 Cor. 1:9). Our union and communion are through the blood of Christ. The Lord's Table is the visible reminder of the blessing we have in union with Jesus. The richness of the symbolism should not be underestimated. Pastor and theologian Joel Beeke writes, "In the Lord's Supper, we partake of the full Christ, feasting on him and his benefits both mentally and spiritually."[7]

Obviously, Christians do not drink the literal blood of Christ when they take the cup of wine at Communion. However, there is much to be understood and received as we hear Christ say, "This is my blood of the covenant, which is poured out for many for the forgiveness of sins" (Matt. 26:28; see Luke 22:20). The poignancy of these words should grip and encourage our hearts every time we hear them. The cup of blessing is a visible and tangible reminder that we are in Christ and Christ in us. It reminds us of the intimate and inseparable union we share with Him. His life and death are ours because His body was broken for us and His blood was shed for us. We are His and He is ours. His blood sealed our union with Him. Every time we come to the Lord's Table, we should be reminded of this wonderful truth.

Why So Much Blood?

Blood runs throughout the Bible. The inevitable question is, "Why so much blood?" It is because there is so much sin in the world. The shedding of blood is the result of sin. In Genesis 9:4, we are told that life is in the blood. If life is in the blood and the blood represents life, then the loss or shedding of blood represents death.[8]

We have no record of the shedding of blood, and no mention of death, before Adam and Eve sinned. But when they committed the greatest of all cosmic treason, they brought not just sin upon the human family, but also death, the shedding of blood.

Consequently, Romans 5:12 reminds us that sin came into the world by Adam, and death through sin, and thus death spread to all men. Sin brought death, and thus the shedding of blood. In fact, it seems God caused the first blood to be shed in response to Adam and Eve's sin. In Genesis 3:21, the Bible says that God, moved by mercy and compassion, made garments of animal skins for Adam and Eve. The implication is that God sacrificed an animal to clothe the man and his wife. Perhaps He even killed the animal before their eyes to demonstrate to them the awful cost of their sin.

If the death of the animal was not demonstrative enough for Adam and Eve, it was not long before death, even the shedding of blood, came right to their home and touched their family in ways they had never imagined. The first instance of the shedding of human blood is recorded in Genesis 4, where we read the tragic story of Adam and Eve's first two sons, Cain and Abel. Cain killed Abel and spilled his blood on the earth. Ironically, Cain's sin was the shedding of Abel's blood, and yet the shedding of blood is the only means by which sin can be removed. In other words, without sin there would be no shedding of blood, but likewise the Bible reminds us that without the shedding of blood, there is no forgiveness of sin (Heb. 9:22). Consequently, in the Scriptures, blood speaks to the need for both retribution and redemption.

Blood Speaks

Consider the death of Abel. As chapter 4 of Genesis begins, we read:

> Now Adam knew Eve his wife, and she conceived and bore Cain, saying, "I have gotten a man with the help of the LORD." And again, she bore his brother Abel. Now Abel was a keeper of sheep, and Cain a worker of the ground. In the course of time Cain brought to the LORD an offering of the fruit of the ground, and Abel also brought of the firstborn of his flock and of their fat portions. And the LORD had regard for Abel and his offering, but for Cain and his offering he had no regard. So Cain was very angry, and his face fell. The LORD said to Cain, "Why are you angry, and why has your face fallen? If you do well, will you not be accepted? And if you do not do well, sin is crouching at the door. Its desire is for you, but you must rule over it." Cain spoke to Abel his brother. And when they were in the field, Cain rose up against his brother Abel and killed him. (Gen. 4:1–8)

After Cain, full of anger and envy, rose up and murdered Abel, God came to Cain and asked him the whereabouts of his younger brother. Cain essentially said to God: "Why are you asking me? I'm not responsible for him." God said that not only was Cain responsible for Abel, but Abel's blood was on Cain's hands. In fact, God told Cain, "The voice of your brother's blood is crying to me from the ground" (v. 10).

Once again, Adam and Eve and their family experienced the penalty for sin, this time in the form of the first human death. Sadly, this death was not that of an intruder, of an escaping criminal, or of a soldier on the battlefield. The horror is that a brother murdered a brother. The wickedness of Cain demonstrated the depth of human depravity and sin.

Cain brought his sacrifice to God, but God refused to accept it. Unlike Abel's sacrifice, Cain's was not made in faith (Heb. 11:4) and lacked a blood atonement for sin. As we have seen, God had established the need for blood atonement, as He had sacrificed an animal to make coverings for Adam and Eve (Gen. 3:21). Commentator and pastor James Montgomery Boice writes:

> Abel's sacrifice involved blood and therefore testified to the death of a substitute. He was coming to God as God had shown he must be approached. When God killed animals in the Garden of Eden and then clothed Adam and Eve with their skins, God was showing that, because sin means death, innocent victims must die in order that sinners might be pardoned. The sacrifice pointed forward to Christ. When Abel came with the offering of blood he was believing God and was looking forward to the provision of the deliverer. When Cain brought his fruit he was rejecting that provision.[9]

Since Cain's sacrifice lacked blood, he decided to use Abel's blood. It was as if he were saying, "God, if you want blood, I'll give you blood!" Abel's faithful sacrifice of a lamb cried out to God for redemption. Cain's wicked sacrifice of Abel cried out for revenge. When the blood of Abel hit the ground, it began to cry out, and God heard it. It cried out for revenge. It cried out for restitution. It cried out for the wrong to be righted. It provided the damning testimony for Cain's condemnation. Cain was guilty of the sin of murder. The blood of Abel stood against him, a stain that Cain could not remove.

Although Abel's blood cried loudly and clearly, it spoke insufficiently. The New Testament tells us, however, that the blood of Christ speaks a better word than the blood of Abel (Heb. 12:24). While Abel's blood cried out for revenge and retribution, the blood of Christ cries out for redemption. When the blood of Jesus hit the ground, it cried not for revenge but for the redemption of the world. As one contemporary songwriter has put it:

Your blood speaks a better word
than all the empty claims
I've heard upon the earth.
Speaks righteousness for me.
It stands in my defense.
Jesus, it's your blood.[10]

This is the power of the blood of Christ in the life of the redeemed. When we behold the blood of Christ, when we have been washed in that blood, our lives are marked out not by revenge but by redemption. How do we know that someone understands the blood of Christ in his life? We know it by the fact that he or she is not out for revenge, but is living out redemption.

It is disheartening to hear Christians, who claim that the blood of Christ has spoken their redemption, speak of revenge. They often feel the need to right every wrong word spoken or wrong deed done against them. Yet, the Bible clearly states in Romans 12:19, "Beloved, never avenge yourselves, but leave it to the wrath of God, for it is written, 'Vengeance is mine, I will repay, says the Lord.'"

At times, we thoughtlessly say, "I just have to get it off of my chest." Or we say, "O, she's going to get hers." However, as a Christian, my cry should never be for revenge, but for redemption. I do not want revenge on my enemies; I want their redemption. I should not pray for their destruction but for their conversion. Why? Because I am covered with the blood of Christ! The blood of Christ speaks a better, a more blessed word than my cry for revenge could ever speak. It says that I am redeemed, and others can be redeemed, too. It says that God did not take His wrath out on me, and thus I should not take mine out on others. Instead of crying for revenge, I must rest in the blood of Christ for redemption. His blood cries out with a louder and more penetrating voice.

Yet, the blood of Christ does more than just cry out—it accomplishes the redemption it proclaims. In the Old Testament, blood spoke loudly. From the murder of Abel to the red-washed doorposts of Israelite homes in Egypt to the sacrificial offerings of bulls and goats by the priests, blood shouted the need for a

Redeemer from the penalty of sin and the pangs of death. In Christ, that Redeemer has come. Through the shedding of His blood, Christ redeemed, once and for all, those who trust and call on Him for salvation. Once and for all, the word of His blood, the word of redemption, speaks on our behalf and declares us free from sin and death. No word in the Scriptures is as loud. No word is as clear. No word is as sweet. It is no wonder we sing:

> *Redeemed, how I love to proclaim it!*
> *Redeemed by the blood of the Lamb;*
> *Redeemed through His infinite mercy,*
> *His child, and forever, I am!*[11]

The blood of the Old Testament spoke, but Christ's blood speaks better. In speaking, it also satisfies.

Blood Satisfies

The Bible is full of epochal events, those grand, earth-altering instances that stand out as high points of redemptive history. In the Old Testament, no event is so dramatic and game-changing as Israel's redemption from Egypt.

In redeeming Israel, God pulled out all the stops. He turned the Nile River to blood. He darkened the sun so that the land was engulfed in perpetual night. He sent an infestation of frogs. If the Egyptians thought that was tolerable, He sent an infestation of gnats (that would have gotten my attention). For those who thought the gnats were not that bad, He sent an infestation of flies (okay, I give up). In all, God sent ten devastating, debilitating, and deathly plagues.

The last plague was the most horrific. God swore to kill the firstborn of every creature in Egypt, including the house of Pharaoh (Ex. 11:4 ff.). So awesome would be the judgment that even the firstborn of Israel would perish unless the Israelites obeyed the commands of God.

To avert the judgment, God commanded every household of Israel to select a male lamb without blemish, kill it, and smear the blood on the doorposts of the house. Then God said: "The blood shall be a sign for you, on the houses where you are. And when I see the blood, I will pass over you, and no plague will befall you to destroy you, when I strike the land of Egypt" (Ex. 12:13).

We must remember that God's wrath was not against Egypt alone for its sin and idolatry, but against Israel as well. God is not a respecter of persons when it comes to the judgment of sin. His judgment was going to wreak havoc not only on the Egyptians but also on the people of Israel—unless they figuratively covered themselves in blood by literally covering their doorposts with it.

What did the blood of the lambs do? It turned away God's wrath and appeased His anger against sin. It satisfied His justice. The blood of the lambs caused God to pass over each house—for a time. The blood satisfied on the night of the Passover, but each year the sacrifices of the lambs had to be made anew. Every year, the sounds of the slaughter of lambs for sacrifices could be heard. For this reason, Israel always longed for an unblemished male lamb who would take way sin once and for all; the One about whom God would say finally, "When I see the blood, I will pass over you *forever*."

When the Lord Jesus Christ came on the scene, He was announced as the Lamb of God who not only takes away our sin (John 1:29) but also turns away God's wrath against us. In fact, 1 Corinthians 5:7 states it plainly to us: "Christ, our Passover lamb, has been sacrificed."

The Israelites lived because of the blood of the lambs that were slain. If you are in Christ, you live because of the blood of the Lamb of God. In the blood of Christ, we have what we lost in Adam, namely, life. The shedding of our Savior's blood was significant not for the blood itself but for what it represents. It represents the perfect, sinless life of Christ poured out unto death for us (Isa. 53:12).

Yet, if all that needed to happen was for Jesus to shed some blood, He could have pricked His finger and placed some blood on the cross or let it spill on the ground, and all would have been well. His precious blood signified His precious life and His precious death. Consequently, the redeemed do not receive a blood transfusion from God. We receive a life transfusion—His death for our death, His life for our life. It all is according to His precious blood, which satisfies God's righteous requirements for life and justice.

Blood in the Old Testament spoke and satisfied. But it did not speak or satisfy well enough. It took the coming of the spotless Lamb of God, whose eternal blood is called precious, priceless, and powerful, to speak and satisfy finally.

In the following pages, allow the Scriptures to show you just how precious the Bible declares our Lord's blood to be. Let it show you the immediate and eternal blessings that are given to those who have been washed in the blood of the Lamb. His blood not only speaks and satisfies, it is totally sufficient. It is no wonder we can sing:

> *O precious blood, which makes us clean,*
> *We trust in it only this hour.*
> *And by our Savior's sacrifice*
> *Now over me sin has lost its power.*[12]

Two

PURCHASED BY THE BLOOD

O victory in Jesus, my Savior, forever.
He sought me and bought me
With His redeeming blood.[13]
— Eugene Bartlett

"Purchasing power" is defined as the amount of goods or services that can be purchased with a unit of currency. When I was a young boy, growing up in rural Michigan, currency was scarce. Whenever I was fortunate enough to get my hands on a dollar, I felt I had the world at my disposal. I would run to the local store and experience real purchasing power. In those days, the stores were stocked with penny candy, and one could buy a bottle of Coca-Cola for a dime. Those were the days. Likewise, I recall my mother driving up to the gas station and saying to the attendant (yes, the gas stations had attendants back then): "Three dollars regular, please." Gas was 40 cents a gallon. Back then, we had greater purchasing power. As the older generation is fond of saying today, "A dollar just ain't what it used to be."

I have since learned that purchasing power can fluctuate. What we are able to afford with a dollar today, we may not be able to afford tomorrow. Many factors affect purchasing power, such as inflation, erratic swings in the stock market, and even one's location in the world. All of these factors and many more cause the value of the currency in our hands to go up or down.

But unlike money, the blood of Christ has purchasing power that is not affected by any of these factors. For instance, this power does not fluctuate depending on where you are in the world. The U.S. dollar may buy more in Canada or the Cayman Islands, but the purchasing power of the blood of Jesus is the same wherever it goes. Our Lord's blood has the same value in Dallas as it has in Darfur. It purchases in Singapore the same thing it purchases in Switzerland. From East Point, Georgia, to East India, our Lord's blood has made eternal purchases.

So, what has God purchased with the blood of Christ? The question actually should be, *whom* has God purchased? According to Scripture, God has purchased the church. The Apostle Paul, on the eve of his departure from Ephesus, gathered the elders and pastors together, and encouraged them to "pay careful attention to yourselves and to all the flock, in which the Holy Spirit has made you overseers, to care for the church of God, which he *obtained* [literally, purchased] *with his own blood*" (Acts 20:28, emphasis added). Paul exhorted the elders and pastors to keep a careful and diligent watch over the church so as to protect it and provide for the general welfare in it. The motivation for this diligence was the fact that the church did not belong to them. They were only stewards of another's property. God had purchased the church with the currency of the blood of His beloved Son, Jesus Christ.

A People for Christ's Own Possession

Likewise, the Bible tells us that the people God purchased by the blood of Jesus are now Jesus' possession. In Titus 2:14, we are reminded that Jesus "gave himself for us to redeem us from all lawlessness and to purify for himself a people for his own possession." Furthermore, in 1 Peter 2:9a, in a description that is reminiscent of Israel in the Old Testament, the Apostle describes the church in the New Testament as "a chosen race, a royal priesthood, a holy nation, a people for his own possession." Thus, Scripture is clear that God, through the blood of Christ, has purchased a people who are now the possession of Jesus.

We understand the nature of possessions. When we purchase something, we expect to take possession of it. We own it. No longer does it belong to the seller. Even when we buy things with credit, such as houses and cars, although we do not really own them and are making payments on them, we treat them as if they are ours. We think, "These are my possessions because I bought them." The Bible says that Christ has paid the price for us. He bought us; therefore, He owns us. Furthermore, He did not purchase His people on credit; He paid in full. We are His.

The fact that the church is Jesus' personal possession is a

powerful motivation for individual hopeful and holy living. Collectively, the church belongs to Jesus. Yet, the collective community is made up of individuals, each of whom has been purchased and redeemed by the blood of Christ. Knowing that we are the possession of Jesus and the dwelling place of the Holy Spirit should provide motivation for our pursuit of holy living in this body. As 1 Corinthians 6:19–20 puts it: "Or do you not know that your body is a temple of the Holy Spirit within you, whom you have from God? You are not your own, for you were bought with a price. So glorify God in your body."

Being the possession of Christ is the hope of the Christian. To be a Christian is to belong to Him. To belong to Christ is the foundation for comfort and security in this life and in the life to come. This is the point poignantly made by Question One, Lord's Day One, of the Heidelberg Catechism. The catechism asks, "What is your only comfort in life and in death?" The answer rings with the truth of the purchasing power of the blood of Christ and our security in His possession:

> That I am not my own, but belong—body and soul, in life and in death—to my faithful Savior Jesus Christ. He has fully paid for all my sins with his precious blood, and has set me free from the tyranny of the devil. He also watches over me in such a way that not a hair can fall from my head without the will of my father in heaven: in fact, all things must work together for my salvation. Because I belong to him, Christ, by his Holy Spirit,

assures me of eternal life and makes me wholeheartedly willing and ready from now on to live for him.

By the precious blood of Christ, we belong to Him. Consequently, the promise and hope for the Christian is not that there will not be bad days. Indeed, trial is eventually the portion of all born into this world (Job 14:1). Yet, if we are born of God, the comfort is that the Lord, who holds the world, holds us, too. When life turns against us and bad days seem to outnumber the good days, the catechism is there to remind us of the surety and faithfulness of our only true comfort. Consider the counsel of one teacher of the catechism:

All things seem to go against you, and it seems that your punishment awaits you every morning. There is "depression" in the land, and in vain do you walk the streets of the city to find employment that you may provide for your family. Whatever savings you were able to lay up for such times are soon consumed. You lose your home. You are forced to live on "relief," or on charity. What is your only comfort? That soon the evil days may be over and prosperity will return to the land? No, but that you belong to Christ! Sickness attacks your frame and day after day, week after week, month after month, you travel a way of suffering. What is your only comfort? That there are physicians and means to alleviate your suffering; or that you may look forward to recovery? No, but your consolation is that you belong to Christ! Death enters your home and takes away a dear child, tearing it from your very heart. And again, your only, mark you well, emphatically your only comfort is that you are not your own, but belong to your faithful Saviour Jesus Christ! . . . Your relationship to Christ is always sufficient.[14]

Praise God! We belong to Jesus because He has purchased us by His blood. He will not return or exchange what He has bought. Yet, we are not just a people for His possession. We are also a flock over which He is the chief Shepherd.

A Flock That Jesus Shepherds

Through His blood, Christ has purchased a large flock of sheep. Sheep are not the smartest animals on the farm. Neither are they the most industrious or the most attractive. Yet, to a good and faithful shepherd, they are his own prized and personal possession, and he guards them with his life.

As we saw above, when Paul addressed the elders and pastors in Ephesus, he told them to watch over and pay careful attention to the "flock" in which they were overseers (Acts 20:28). The implication is that the elders were part of the flock. Though they were to oversee it, they were not detached from it. That means they did not own it. They were stewards of Jesus' possession, and as sheep themselves, they were possessed by Jesus as well. They did not purchase the sheep; God did. Consequently, Christ expects to find His flock well fed and accounted for when He returns.

The Bible makes clear that God sees the people He has purchased by Jesus' blood as His sheep. In Psalm 100:3, we are reminded: "Know that the LORD, he is God! It is he who made us, and we are his; we are his people, and the sheep of his pasture." Here we see that we belong to God because He made us. Yet, His possession of us is not only through our creation, but also through our redemption. For example, when Christ declared Himself to be the Good Shepherd, He did so acknowledging possession of sheep for whom He would lay down His life: "I am the good shepherd. I know my own and my own know me, just as the Father knows me and I know the Father; and I lay down my life for the sheep" (John 10:14–15). Jesus gave His life for the sheep. He shed His blood so that He would secure the flock of God. It is this flock that elders and pastors are to oversee, knowing that the flock ultimately is the possession of Christ, the chief Shepherd (1 Peter 5:4).

Our Lord's blood has purchasing power, not only to obtain us but also to cleanse us, wash us, sanctify us, and to make us righteous and holy. We must remember that heaven does not deal in dollars, pounds, pesos, Euros, or even gold or silver. The only currency that is of value in heaven and throughout eternity is the blood of Christ. It is the only currency that can get us in. It is, as the songwriter says, our victory in Jesus:

> *O victory in Jesus,*
> *My Savior, forever.*
> *He sought me and bought me*
> *With His redeeming blood;*

He loved me ere I knew Him,
And all my love is due Him.
He plunged me to victory
Beneath the cleansing flood.[15]

There is a popular credit-card company that likes to ask in its commercials, "What's in your wallet?" Wouldn't it be interesting if, when we get to heaven, someone were standing at the gate asking, "What's in your wallet?" At that point, dollars won't do. Euros won't count. Silver and gold will be of no service. You had better have Jesus. You had better have His blood. "What's in your wallet?" Your answer must be: "The blood of Jesus! He has purchased me, so I am His and He is mine forever."

Three
___

PROPITIATION
BY THE BLOOD

Unto the blood of sprinkling come,
Where better things of Him are said;
The Lamb of God was crucified,
My sins placed there upon His head.[16]
—TONY CARTER

The theology of the church is filled with big words, such as *justification, sanctification, predestination,* and others. These big words carry big meanings. These big meanings reveal to us the bigness of our God and the greatness of our salvation.

One such word is *propitiation.* Propitiation is not a term that easily flows from our lips. You probably will not find it the topic of conversation at your next church social. It likely will not come up at the barbershop or hair salon. Unfortunately, it probably is not the subject of too many Sunday school classes, either. Yet, while it is not a popular topic of conversation, its importance to the Christian faith cannot be overstated. J. I. Packer, in his classic book *Knowing God*, asks, "Has the word propitiation any place in your Christianity?"[17] It does, whether we know it or not. At the heart of the work of Christ is His sacrificial outpouring of His blood, which, the Bible states, provides a propitiation for our sins (Rom. 3:25).

One of the most familiar and important verses in the Bible reads, "For all have sinned and fall short of the glory of God" (Rom. 3:23). However, the verses that follow are even more important. They tell us that those who have sinned are now freely and graciously made right with God through Jesus Christ: "[They] are justified by his grace as a gift, through the redemption that is in Christ Jesus, whom God put forward as a *propitiation by his blood,* to be received by faith. This was to show God's righteousness" (vv. 24–25a, emphasis added). We all stood justly condemned because of sin. Yet God was pleased to offer Christ as a propitiation, and this through the shedding of His blood.

What is a propitiation? William Hendricksen defines a propitiation as a "wrath-removing sacrifice."[18] In accordance with His holiness, God is angry at sin (Ps. 7:11). Sin is rebellion against God's will, the manifestation of humanity's revolt against its Creator. It has been said that sin is not just breaking the rules, it is making one's own rules. Though God is patient and kind, He will not leave the guilty unpunished (Ex. 34:7). Those who are guilty of sinning need God's wrath against their sins to be removed and His justice to be satisfied. Jesus, in giving His life as a sacrifice, satisfied the righteous and just wrath of God against our sin, thus providing for us reconciliation and peace with God.

To understand the importance of the propitiating work of Christ on our behalf, we must understand the place and purpose of God's wrath against sin. We naturally expect people to be angry at wrong. Former President George W. Bush was very popular when he took action after the 9/11 terrorist attacks. When he showed his displeasure and vowed to bring the wrath of America down upon the offending terrorists, his popularity went through the roof. Mr. Bush was angry at the terrorism of Al Qaeda—and America applauded. Even more so, God is filled with righteous anger and indignation against the terrorism of humanity toward His righteousness and holiness. Yet there is no applause. However, God has more right to be angry at the sin of the world than we have at a thousand terrorists. The Bible does not hesitate to remind us of this, and to show that God's anger is right and just.

Scripture says that God's righteous wrath is against "all ungodliness and unrighteousness of men" (Rom. 1:18). He is angry toward those who make excuses for or dismiss their sins and the sins of others (Rom. 1:32). God's wrath is against the unrepentant, those who thumb their noses at Him with no shame for doing so (Rom. 2:5). God is rightly wrathful toward all manner of sin (Col. 3:5–6). Furthermore, God's wrath is against all humanity, because all have sinned (Rom. 3:23). The result of sin is the compromise and defilement of God's original design for creation. Therefore, He has a right to be angry.

Most of us are far too familiar with anger. Often, it is our own anger rather than the anger of others that causes us the most trouble. Yet, it is our own anger that we are least likely to know or understand. One theologian, in raising the question of anger, wrote: "What is anger? Many of us might say, 'I can't define it, but I know it when I see it, especially if it's directed toward me.'"[19] Indeed, I am usually ready to decry all fits of anger and indignation directed toward me, but I am less likely to be so definite when judging the anger in my own heart, and how it is expressed against others.

"Why are you so angry?" This is the question I asked a young man as we counseled concerning the bitter division between him and his wife and children. "I don't know," was his reply. The more we talked, the more we discovered that his anger had no biblical justification. We sinful human beings get angry, but we rarely have good reason for it. In fact, the Bible reminds us that the wrath and anger of man does not produce the righteousness of God (James 1:20). Thus, we are told to put it away (Col. 3:8).

Yet, while our anger does not produce the righteousness of God, the Bible says that the wrath of God brings forth the righteousness that He requires (Rom. 3:25). Clearly, the purpose of God's wrath is to demonstrate the awfulness of sin and consequently to magnify the glory of His grace that is ours in the forgiveness of sin through faith in Jesus Christ.

The Purpose of God's Wrath

The wrath of God is a righteous indignation that brings about the redemption of His people. The Bible tells us that because of the wrath of God, His righteousness has been revealed apart from the law (Rom. 3:21). God's wrath is for the purpose of pointing people to His mercy in Christ. His anger against sin reminds us that we are not righteous, that we stand in need of righteousness.

The righteousness we need has two important aspects to it. First, according to the Scriptures, the righteousness we need is "apart from the law" (Rom. 3:21). Our efforts to keep the law of God will not accomplish the righteous requirement of God. In giving the law through Moses, God revealed how unrighteous humanity is. In all honesty, we are all law-breakers. Yes, some are lesser thieves than others, but we are all thieves. We have all stolen God's glory in some fashion (Rom. 3:23). Yes, some are lesser liars than others, but all liars are liable to eternal judgment (Rev. 21:8). The Bible clearly states that there is not one righteous person—"no, not one" (Rom. 3:10). Through His law, God says do, but we do not. God says do not, but we do. Who can say he has never offended any aspect of God's holy law? The rich young ruler foolishly claimed to have kept all of God's commands from his childhood. Yet, Christ exposed his hypocrisy (Luke 18:18ff.), reminding us that even what we perceive to be our most righteous deeds are marred, tainted, and worthless in the sight of God (Isa. 64:6). Our ability to keep the law is far too inadequate to make us right with God. Therefore, it is necessary for us to look somewhere else—even outside of ourselves.

That brings us to the all-important second aspect to this righteousness. The righteousness we need is not only "apart from the law," but more important, it is "by faith." The righteousness we need to turn God's anger to blessing is not of our own doing, but is a righteousness that comes to us by faith in the finished work of Christ. The blood of Christ is our propitiation—the wrath-removing sacrifice. Faith is the means by which we receive that sacrifice as our righteousness. This is what the Christian rapper Shai Linne means when he tells us:

> *Just fall back, and with the eyes of faith*
> *Behold the beauty of surprising grace,*
> *Because the Lamb has died, third day He had to rise;*
> *He's magnified, God's wrath is satisfied.*[20]

Still, though faith is important, we must remember that it is not ultimate. It is not faith that turns away God's wrath and anger against sin; it is the blood of Christ. It is not faith that saves; it is the finished work of Christ. Admittedly, faith is important. We cannot be saved without faith. However, it is Christ who saves, not faith. While faith brings the righteousness of Christ to us, it is the righteousness of Christ that actually earns us God's pleasure.

God's Wrath Is Propitiated by Christ

The blessed truth is that Christ, by His blood—His life and death—has taken God's wrath and punishment for us. When Christ was on the cross, He not only took the punishment due for our sin, He took the wrath of God, the righteous indignation associated with the punishment.

Since there is no more sin, there is no more wrath. If you are a Christian, the blood of Christ is your propitiation. God is not angry with you, nor will He be again. This is the amazing propitiating power of the blood of Christ. If you are a Christian, your mother or father may get angry with you, but not God. Your wife or husband may get angry with you, but not God. You may get angry with yourself or, worse yet, find yourself in the senseless position of being angry with God. Yet this does not, and will not, move God to be angry with you. This is why we can come to God without fear of condemnation (Rom. 8:1).

To say that God is not angry and will never be angry with those who are in Christ is not to say that God will not deal with sin in our lives. God does discipline His people. Like any good parent, God chastises His children when necessary. In fact, the Bible clearly speaks of God's discipline of those whom He loves:

> "For the Lord disciplines the one he loves, and chastises every son whom he receives." It is for discipline that you have to endure. God is treating you as sons. For what son is there whom his father does not discipline? If you are left without discipline, in which all have participated, then you are illegitimate children and not sons. Besides this, we have had earthly fathers who disciplined us and we respected them. Shall we not much more be subject to the Father of spirits and live? For they disciplined us for a short time as it seemed best to them, but he disciplines us for our good, that we may share his holiness. For the moment all discipline seems painful rather than pleasant, but later it yields the peaceful fruit of righteousness to those who have been trained by it. (Heb. 12:6–11)

29

Though God's discipline is upon those He loves, His discipline is never out of anger. My wife and I have committed ourselves to disciplining our children, but we try never to chastise them out of anger. We are not always successful because of the sinfulness and inconsistency in our hearts. God, however, does not have that problem—His chastisement of His children is always without anger: "My son, do not despise the LORD's discipline or be weary of his reproof, for the LORD reproves him whom he loves, as a father the son in whom he delights" (Prov. 3:11–12).

In the New Testament, the wrath and righteous anger of God is never toward His redeemed. It is never mentioned as against those in Christ. Rather, it is against the "sons of disobedience" (Eph. 5:6); those in sin, not those in Christ (Col. 3:5–7). In fact, because we are in Christ, we are not the objects of God's wrath in this life or the life to come (1 Thess. 5:9). The blood of Christ has propitiated God's righteous anger against our sin.

If God has poured out His wrath against sin on Christ on the cross, He cannot also pour it out on us. Again, this is why we can come to God without fear of condemnation. One of my favorite hymn writers is Augustus Toplady. Of his hymns, my favorite may be "From Whence This Fear and Unbelief," which speaks so eloquently and clearly of the sufficient propitiatory and atoning work of Christ. Toplady reminded us that Christ has offered the wrath-removing sacrifice, and so we need not fear—only believe:

> *From whence this fear and unbelief?*
> *Hath not the Father put to grief*
> *His spotless Son for me?*

And will the righteous Judge of men
Condemn me for that debt of sin
Which, Lord, was charged on Thee?

Complete atonement Thou hast made,
And to the utmost Thou has paid
Whate'er Thy people owed;
How then can wrath on me take place,
If sheltered in Thy righteousness,
And sprinkled with Thy blood?

If thou has my discharge procured
And freely in my room endured
The whole of wrath divine;
Payment God cannot twice demand,
First at my bleeding Surety's hand,
And then again at mine.[21]

Four

JUSTIFIED BY THE BLOOD

Bearing shame and scoffing rude,
In my place condemned He stood,
Sealed my pardon with His blood:
Hallelujah! What a Savior![22]
— PHILIP P. BLISS

Have you ever wondered why God loves you and desires you in His eternal blessed presence? Have you ever contemplated (seriously) why God would look favorably on you and bless you rather than condemn you? Most of us (dare I say, all of us?) think more highly of ourselves than we ought. While very few of us would admit it, we live our lives as if there is something about us that makes God want to be our friend.

Amazingly, we treat God like one of our earthly friends. We cannot help ourselves. We know why we like our friends and, to some degree, why they like us. We treat them in certain ways and do certain things so that they will continue to like us. In many regards, this is how we relate to God. We believe that if we do this or do not do that, then God will like us. He must. After all, what is there not to love?

Well, the Apostle Paul would answer that question by saying, "Everything." The human condition is not just a bucket of errors; it is an ocean of iniquity. Our condition could be summed up by something akin to Murphy's Law: Whatever *could* be wrong with humanity *is* wrong.

Someone once wrote: "I never had a slice of bread, particularly large and wide, that did not fall upon the floor, and always on the buttered side."[23] Such is the state of humanity in relation to God. Humanity is in a perpetual, ever-deepening abyss of separation from God because of sin and rebellion. The better humanity tries to make itself, the more offensive it becomes to God (Isa. 64:6). Talk about seemingly irreconcilable differences! This problem poses the greatest question ever faced by the human race, namely, "How can sinful, rebellious human beings stand accepted and loved in the presence of God?" In other words, how are we ever to be reconciled to a holy and righteous God? How are we ever to be made right with God and reclaim what Adam and Eve lost? In other words, how are we to be justified?

The Bible reminds us that our justification is secured only by the blood of Christ. In Romans 5:6–9, Paul writes:

> For while we were still weak, at the right time Christ died for the ungodly. For one will scarcely die for a righteous

person—though perhaps for a good person one would dare even to die—but God shows his love for us in that while we were still sinners, Christ died for us. Since, therefore, we have now been *justified by his blood*, much more shall we be saved by him from the wrath of God. (Emphasis added)

Justification is God's declaration that sinners are in a right and acceptable relationship with Him based solely on the person and work of Jesus Christ, the benefits of which are received by faith alone. According to R. C. Sproul:

Justification may be defined as that act by which unjust sinners are made right in the sight of a just and holy God. The supreme need of unjust persons is righteousness. It is this lack of righteousness that is supplied by Christ on behalf of the believing sinner. Justification by faith alone means justification by the righteousness or merit of Christ alone, not by our goodness or good deeds.[24]

Justification is the declaration that those who were once enemies of God are now, through faith in Christ, friends and beloved. Justification does not come to good people, or even to righteous people, but to those who are at odds with God. We might be inclined to justify our friends and family. We might even be inclined to justify someone we think useful and valuable to society. However, according to the Bible, God justifies those who believe through the blood of Christ.

For Whom Did Christ Die?

The question is often raised, "For whom did Christ die?" In Romans 5:6–9, the Bible tells us that Christ died for those who are "weak," "ungodly," and "sinners." "Weak" speaks to our inability to save ourselves. It indicates that we are without strength and power. It brings to mind someone who is incurably sick. The illness has debilitated him to such a degree that all power of recovery has left him and death is inevitable. He is unable to save himself from this pending end. Jesus declared that these are the ones He came to save (Mark 2:17). As weak spiritual invalids, we not only could not save ourselves, we had no idea that a cure was possible.

"Ungodly" speaks to our activity in opposition to the ways of God. It is the designation of sinners as impious, refusing to worship the God who created them while living and loving contrary to His holy character and commands. It is reflective of what the Bible means when, speaking collectively of humanity, it says: "None is righteous, no, not one; no one understands; no one seeks for God. All have turned aside; together they have become worthless; no one does good, not even one.' . . . 'There is no fear of God before their eyes'" (Rom. 3:10–12, 18). Thess verses remind us that the weak and the ungodly are such because they are sinners—transgressors of God's law.

"Sinners" is the summation of what we are in relation to God's Word and will. The Westminster Shorter Catechism defines sin as "any lack of conformity unto, or transgression of, the law of God."[25] Sin is manifested when we do what God commands us not to do and when we fail to do what God has commanded us to do. Since the fall of Adam and Eve, humanity has been in a downward spiral of sin. We have moved further and further away from God and His laws. Consequently, the greatest advancements in human history have not been in medicine, science, or technology, but in humanity's ability and willingness to sin against God. This is not an assessment of those we would deem to be the worst of us; this is the condition of every man, woman, and child: "All have sinned and fall short of the glory God" (Rom. 3:23).

Remarkably, it is such people whom Christ came to save. Jesus died to save the weak (those who could not save themselves), the ungodly (those who did not even know they needed to be saved), and sinners (the weak and ungodly who live in open rebellion against God's Word and will).

As the Bible plainly states, "Christ died for the ungodly" (Rom. 5:6). Here are five of the most heart-humbling, awe-inspiring, and joy-producing words we will ever hear. As many have said, "Here is the gospel in five words." Those who are justified are those who willingly admit to being ungodly, and thus are willing to trust in Christ alone for their godliness. They understand that their ungodliness is such that self-justification is not possible.

Most of us abhor self-justification when we hear it in others. Excuses like, "Well, that's just the way I am," "I couldn't help myself," or even, "The Devil made me do it" do not carry much weight in the courts of our land. These excuses carry even less weight and validity in the courts of heaven. We have often heard it said, "The one who serves as his own attorney has a fool for a client." If this is true in our courts, how much more true is it in the courts of heaven? Self-defense may be plausible when we are standing before human judges. It is self-destructive when we stand before God.

Job understood this when he asked, "But how can a man be in the right before God?" (Job 9:2). Self-justification is not the answer. As Job went on to say, "If one wished to contend with [God], one could not answer him once in a thousand times" (v. 3). Even more than we do, God abhors self-justification. Yet, God does not simply abhor self-justification; He graciously has provided a way of justification outside of ourselves. We need not try to justify ourselves, for God has provided a justification by faith. We need not plead our case with God, for He has provided Christ as our Advocate (1 John 2:1). Jesus' blood pleads for us. He is the Advocate and His blood is the plea. Ours is only the faith to trust Him. As the songwriters remind us:

> *Let Your blood plead for me,*
> *Let Your blood wash me clean.*
> *I believe, Lord, I believe*
> *Your blood has covered me.*[26]

At the heart of this gospel is the blood of Christ, which secures our justification. It pleads our case and secures our pardon.

Why Did Christ Die?

Furthermore, the Bible reminds us that our justification is grounded in the love of God. The answer to the question "For whom did Christ die?" hints at the answer to the question "Why did Christ die?" but it does not fully explain it. Why did Christ die for us? Yes, He died because we needed to be saved. But even more glorious is that He died to demonstrate God's love in saving us. Our salvation is not a disinterested, detached act of God. On the contrary, it is an act of compassionate, saving love. Christ died to show the all-surpassing, incomparable height, depth, width, and length of God's love for us.

Tina Turner once asked the question, "What's love got to do with it?" Again, Paul would answer by saying, "Everything!" At the heart of our salvation is the love of God. We are not redeemed without it. This redeeming love is threefold. It is the love the Son shows for the Father in submitting to the will of God in the redemption of His people. It is the love the Father shows for the Son in redeeming a people who will ultimately be conformed to the image of the Son. It is the love the Father and the Son show for God's people in redeeming us at all cost (John 3:16; Gal. 2:20). It's a love triangle. But unlike the love triangles we know, this one works, bringing joy and delight to all. The songwriter captured it well:

> The love of God is greater far than tongue or pen can ever tell.
> It goes beyond the highest star, and reaches to the lowest hell.
> The guilty pair, bowed down with care, God gave His son
> to win.
> His erring child He reconciled, and pardoned from his sin.[27]

The Puritans would say, "God's love is an ocean without floor and without shore." This is the height, depth, width, and length of God's love: *Christ died for us.*

In the previous chapter, we saw that through the blood of Christ in propitiation, justice goes up to God's court. Now we see that through the blood of Christ in justification, love comes down to us. Love came down in Jesus Christ. To demonstrate the depth of the Father's love, Christ left heaven. He laid aside His glory, concealing His majesty (Phil. 2:6–7). He subjected Himself to the creature's scorn, outcast from a world He created. He suffered demonic attack, lies, and public ridicule. Friends forsook Him. He was brutally beaten, stripped, and put to open shame. Spat upon and slapped, publicly and shamefully executed, He assumed the guilt and punishment for every sin we ever committed. He reconciled us to God and secured our acceptance before God. Why? Because justice demanded it and our justification required it. Communion with God is impossible for us without it. He did it because He loved us.

The relationship that was lost because of Adam has been restored in Christ. The peace that was forfeited in Adam has been regained in Christ. In Adam, we stood condemned. In Christ, we stand justified, because He loved us even before we knew Him or understood what He was doing (Rom. 5:6).

Thankfully, now we know, and that knowledge is the sweetness and glory of our song:

> *How deep the Father's love for us,*
> *How vast beyond all measure;*
> *that He should give His only Son*
> *to make a wretch His treasure.*[28]

Five
—

REDEEMED
BY THE BLOOD

E'er since by faith I saw the stream
Your flowing wounds supply,
Redeeming love has been my theme,
And shall be till I die.[29]
— William Cowper

Cecil B. DeMille's *The Ten Commandments* (1956) is one of the most successful movies ever made. At the time, it was an epic cinematic achievement. Its cinematography and special effects wowed the movie world. Everyone marveled, not only at the presentation, but also at the story itself. The story indeed is a grand one, as it recapitulates the entire drama of redemption. The deliverance of the children of Israel from slavery in Egypt is both an unforgettable episode in God's purposeful and powerful salvation of His people, and a powerful foreshadowing of the redemption to come in Christ. Just as God redeemed the Israelites from Egypt through the blood of the lambs on their doorposts, so all God's people ultimately are redeemed through the blood of Jesus Christ, the Lamb of God.

This truth is expressed very simply in Ephesians 1:7, where we see that in Christ "we have *redemption through his blood*, the forgiveness of our trespasses, according to the riches of his grace" (emphasis added). We have this blessed redemption through the blood of Christ because God chose us in Him "before the foundation of the world" (v. 4) and predestined us (v. 5) to receive it.

Redemption Draws Near

Nothing says salvation like "redemption." The word literally means a release effected or brought about by the payment of a ransom or price. We know what it is to redeem something. We redeem coupons, stamps, credit-card points, and frequent-flyer miles. In order to redeem these items and receive the benefits of them, we must have paid a price for them. When the Bible says that we have been redeemed, it means that we have been delivered, rescued, purchased, and ransomed by and for God. Redeemed from what? Redeemed from slavery to sin (Rom. 6:19–20).

One of the major themes of redemption in the Bible is the idea of captivity. The idea is that someone is trapped, enslaved, kidnapped, or held captive, and thus a price must be paid or a sacrifice made in order to rescue him. When it comes to our redemption through Christ, we were in a situation similar to Israel. As Israel was enslaved in Egypt, we were enslaved to sin and death.

When Adam and Eve sinned in the garden of Eden, they sold themselves and all their progeny into slavery—slavery to sin and death. From this captivity, there is no escape by natural means. The power of sin is such that it has mastery over its subjects even to the point of death (1 Cor. 15:56). Those who admit to addictions understand this well. Yet, biblically speaking, we were all addicts at one time. Drugs, alcohol, sex, pornography, and food are controlling and addictive forces for sin, but they are not the only ones. Money, popularity, pride, gossip, work, and ambition can all become sinfully addictive and hold us captive to the destruction of our souls.

Thus, it is important to see that the Bible portrays sin not just as an action but also as a tyrannical master (Rom. 6:16). Jesus said in John 8:34, "Everyone who practices sin is a slave to sin." Elsewhere, the Bible reminds us that all who are of the flesh are "sold under sin" (Rom. 7:14). Sin is a power that must be broken. It is a tyrant that must be defeated.

This is the condition that all people are in prior to faith in Christ. We come into the world held captive by sin. We live every day according to the edicts of our master and in accordance with our captivity. The human race apart from Christ is hopelessly and helplessly held captive in sin's dark night. However, when faith in Christ is realized, our condition changes—we are brought to the light of His grace.

If you are a Christian today, you have been redeemed—you have been purchased, delivered, and rescued. The Bible says sin no longer has mastery over you (Rom. 6:12, 17–18). Just as Pharaoh ceased to hold power over the children of Israel after their deliverance, so sin no longer has power over you. The blood of Christ has delivered you from captivity to sin and death. People make much of so-called "deliverance ministries," and some of those ministries go so far as to call themselves "deliverance churches." True deliverance, however, is found in the blood of Christ, which has redeemed us from sin. Every true church is a deliverance church if it is preaching salvation and redemption through Jesus Christ our Lord.

Consequently, the Bible teaches us that we have been purchased with a price (1 Cor. 7:23)—the precious, priceless blood of Christ. Seeing that we have such a great redemption, the Bible says we are to glorify the One who has purchased us. And yet, the purchase is all the more glorious when we realize it is because we were chosen in Christ and predestined in love that we have been redeemed by His blood.

Chosen to Be Saints

The word translated as "chose" in Ephesians 1:4 is the Greek word *eklegomai*. It is a word also translated as "to elect or select." We understand this idea in the United States, as we are always in the process of evaluating candidates for public office. Yet, when the Bible speaks of election, it is not talking about the choice of presidents, mayors, or city council members. Biblical election is the sovereign act of God in choosing sinners to be saints. By comparison, human election is conditional—we elect those we like, who hold our values. God's election is unconditional—before anyone is able to do good or bad, God chooses those upon whom He determines to show His saving love (Rom. 9:11–13). Someone has rightly said: "We don't get to choose our family. We do get to choose our friends." God chooses both His family and His friends.

While the subject of election has been the source of numerous debates between Christians, the fact that God has elected us should not be a point of contention as much as a reason for praise. When the Bible speaks of election, it does so to give glory to God and comfort to His people. The often-quoted Romans 8:28—"And we know that for those who love God all things work together for good, for those who are called according to his purpose"—appears in the context of the Apostle Paul's teaching on God's electing and predestining purposes. This verse has served as a balm for many anxious and troubled Christians.

Yet, to understand it rightly is to understand not only that God is working out all things well, but also to understand why. Why are all things working for our good? The reason is that God has been, is, and forever will be in control of all things, including our destinies. As the Scriptures go on to say: "For those whom he foreknew he also predestined to be conformed to the image of his Son. . . . And those whom he predestined he also called, and those whom he called he also justified, and those whom he justified he also glorified" (Rom. 8:29–30). All things work together for good because our lives are not left up to chance. They are in the hands of our electing, sovereign God. Wayne Grudem writes:

> From eternity to eternity God has acted with the good of his people in mind. But if God has always acted for our

good and will in the future act for our good, Paul reasons, then will he not also in our present circumstances work every circumstance together for our good as well? In this way predestination is seen as a comfort for believers in the everyday events of life. [30]

God's sovereign election is a sweet and awe-inspiring truth. As the hymn writer reminds us:

How sweet and awful is the place
With Christ within the doors,
While everlasting love displays
The choicest of her stores.

Why was I made to hear thy voice,
And enter while there's room,
When thousands make a wretched choice,
And rather starve than come?

'Twas the same love that spread the feast
That sweetly drew us in;
Else we had still refused to taste,
And perished in our sin. [31]

According to the Bible, our election was according to God's predetermined plan. Election is the way God would have it to be. It is a demonstration of His love. This is the way of redemption that brings us most comfort and God most glory. Pastor and theologian Sinclair Ferguson reminds us of how we should consider these biblical truths:

> When we begin to think about the biblical doctrines of election and predestination in this light, we will feel some measure of the thrill, which the writers of the New Testament did whenever they wrote about it. For them these truths were not controversial but joyful. They saw that if they were united to Christ, this meant that in choosing Christ and loving him God had also chosen them![32]

Predestined in Love

Thankfully, God does not leave our lives, or our salvation, in our hands. If He were to let us determine the courses of our lives in this world apart from Him, we would never choose Him. Because of innate sin and our irrepressible inclination toward it, we would never turn to God. We would never seek Him. Because we are all "under sin," the Bible says: "None is righteous, no, not one; no one understands; no one seeks for God. All have turned aside; together they have become worthless; no one does good, not even one" (Rom. 3:10–12). Yet, because God has predestined us to glory and a relationship with Himself, we do not remain in this condition of alienation from Him.

We are told that those whom God has chosen, He has predestined in love. Predestination can be difficult for us to grasp. Because it is difficult, it also often becomes controversial. As one author has said, "There are two things about the doctrine of predestination that cannot be gainsaid: it is important and it is controversial."[33] The importance of this doctrine is seen in how the Bible ties it to the love of God. Our God is a loving God. Yet, He is also a predestining God. When these two truths are put together, we see just how wonderfully, powerfully, and eternally God has loved us.

His predestining love for us has many descriptive dimensions to it. His predestining love is demonstrated in that we are adopted into His family (Eph. 1:5). His predestining love is at work in that we are being made over into the glorious image of the risen Christ (Rom. 8:29). His predestining love guarantees that we are the recipients of eternal life (Acts 13:48). So, contrary to some opinions, God's predestining grace is not without affection. On the contrary, it flows out of His inexpressible love: "Yet the LORD set his heart in love on your fathers and chose their offspring after them, you above all peoples, as you are this day" (Deut. 10:15).

While some may characterize predestination as the doctrine of an unmoved tyrant, the Bible tells us that predestination is an exercise of the divine heart full of love: "In love he predestined us for adoption as sons through Jesus Christ, according to the purpose of his will, to the praise of his glorious grace, with which he has blessed us in the Beloved. In him we have redemption through his blood, the forgiveness of our trespasses, according to the riches of his grace" (Eph. 1:4b–7). God in love predetermined that we would be members of His family through the redemptive blood of Christ. In other words, those whom He redeems from sin, He adopts into His family. The redeemed who were once in bondage to sin are now sons and daughters of God.

This is the blessed privilege of the redeemed. This is the glory of the Redeemer.

There Is a Redeemer

Psalm 107:2 says, "Let the redeemed of the LORD say so, whom he hath redeemed from the hand of the enemy" (KJV). Has He redeemed you from sin and death? Say it! Has He redeemed you from guilt and shame? Say it! Has He redeemed your life from the pains and penalties of sin in this world and the world to come? Say it!

Furthermore, do you long and look forward to the final redemption, when your humble estate will give way to the glorious revelation of our Redeemer at His second coming? Do you long for the day when your faith shall be sight and the clouds be rolled back as a scroll? Then Jesus says in Luke 21:28, "Raise your heads, because your redemption is drawing near!" Who is our redemption? The songwriter reminds us:

There is a Redeemer, Jesus God's own Son.
Precious Lamb of God, Messiah, Holy One.[34]

Six

BROUGHT NEAR BY THE BLOOD

Jesus sought me when a stranger,
Wand'ring from the fold of God;
He, to rescue me from danger,
Interposed His precious blood.[35]
—ROBERT ROBINSON

Men are prone to forget things that women hold most dear. Many husbands even have forgotten the dates of anniversaries or birthdays. Most of them have experienced the wrath of their wives' glances when, in polite company, they failed to recall—with joy—important occasions. I, too, have been the recipient of that unfortunate stare.

Yet I would contend that forgetfulness is a malady that is no respecter of gender or person. It befalls us all. God knows this, and thus He graciously calls us time and time again to remember.

Faithful preaching reminds us of the glory of the resurrected Christ: "Remember Jesus Christ, risen from the dead, the offspring of David, as preached in my gospel" (2 Tim. 2:8). The songs we sing remind us of God's amazing grace, mercy, and love. When we come to the Lord's Table, we remember that we are in covenant with Him and that He promises to receive us one day. The Apostle Paul writes:

> For I received from the Lord what I also delivered to you, that the Lord Jesus on the night when he was betrayed took bread, and when he had given thanks, he broke it, and said, "This is my body which is for you. Do this in remembrance of me." In the same way also he took the cup, after supper, saying, "This cup is the new covenant in my blood. Do this, as often as you drink it, in remembrance of me." For as often as you eat this bread and drink the cup, you proclaim the Lord's death until he comes. (1 Cor. 11:23–26)

Yet it appears that nothing is more important for us to remember than our former lives and how we who were not beloved became beloved of God (Rom. 9:25) through the person and work—indeed, through the blood—of Jesus Christ. Paul tells us: "Remember that you were at that time separated from Christ, alienated from the commonwealth of Israel and strangers to the covenants of promise, having no hope and without God in the world. But now in Christ Jesus you who once were far off have been *brought near by the blood of Christ*" (Eph. 2:12–13, emphasis added).

Like the Ephesians, we are called to remember where we were when the blood of Christ came to us so that we might better appreciate where we are now. Here is how John R. W. Stott puts it:

> There are some things which Scripture tells us to forget (like the injuries which others do to us). But there is one thing in particular which we are commanded to remember and never to forget. This is what we were before God's love reached down and found us. For only if we remember our former alienation (distasteful as some of it may be to us), shall we be able to remember the greatness of the grace which forgave and is transforming us.[36]

Such We Were

Chapter two of Ephesians opens with a sobering recollection of the condition of all people before they come to know Christ. We are described as: dead in trespasses and sins; followers of the Devil; sons and daughters of disobedience; given over to and controlled by fleshy lusts and desires; and by nature under the wrath of God for our innate, willful disregard for Him. This is not the state of a few bad people in the world. This is the state of all humanity apart from Christ (Eph. 2:1–3). In fact, everyone comes into the world SDOA (spiritually dead on arrival). Apart from Christ, life is nothing more than a march from the womb to the tomb. It is not pretty.

Yet in verse 4, Paul makes a transition from what we all were to what God did for us in Christ. Through the richness of His mercy, God made those who were dead in sin alive in Christ. By grace through faith, those who were children of wrath have been raised up with Christ and adopted into the family of God, so they now are children of God, with all the privileges and blessings of sons and daughters. Those who were once under the wrath of God for their disobedience are now trophies of His grace, and even evidence of God's gracious handiwork, designed in Christ to do the good works of God (vv. 5–10).

Having detailed the riches of God's grace in saving lost, disobedient sinners and adopting them as sons and daughters, Paul then enjoins all Christians, but especially Gentiles, to remember their former state: separated from Christ, alienated from the commonwealth, strangers to the covenants, having no hope, and without God. William Hendricksen describes this condition as "Christless, stateless, friendless, hopeless, and Godless."[37]

First, Paul says, we were once "separated from Christ." In chapter one of Ephesians, Paul lays out all the spiritual blessings that belong to those who are "in Christ." Union with Christ is the source of the Christian's joy and faith. In fact, the greatest comfort offered to the Christian is the knowledge and promise that nothing or no one can "separate us from the love of God in Christ Jesus our Lord" (Rom. 8:39). Yet, before we received Christ, this joy and comfort were foreign to us. We were separated from Christ, and none of the blessings of union with Him belong to those who are separated from Him. Have we forgotten that such we were?

Second, we were once "alienated from the commonwealth

of Israel and strangers to the covenants of promise." We flew the flag of an enemy power. We wore the colors of a defiant and rebellious people. During the gang wars between the Crips and the Bloods that ravaged parts of Los Angeles in the 1980s, a person could lose his life simply by wearing a red scarf or do-rag in a blue neighborhood, or a blue scarf or do-rag in a red neighborhood. The rapper Ice-T captured this ethos when he described his hometown as:

South Central L.A., home of the body bag;
You wanna die, wear the wrong color rag.[38]

Before Christ, we wore the wrong rag. We lived under the wrong colors. We flew the wrong flag. We were "alienated from the life of God" (Eph. 4:18). Consequently, as those in rebellion to God, we were counted dead and under the penalty of death.

As those who were outside of Christ, we had no portion in His inheritance. Though we may have had friends in this world, the friendship of God was beyond our reach. We were strangers to the true God and outsiders even while often living next door to God's covenant people.

It is to these strangers that the blood of Christ comes. The hymn writer is right:

Jesus sought me when a stranger,
Wand'ring from the fold of God;
He, to rescue me from danger,
Interposed His precious blood.[39]

We were in danger from sin, but even more dreadful, from the wrath of God. Have we forgotten that such we were?

Third, we were once without "hope and without God in the world." Even though we may have had a desire for a better life now and a blissful eternal existence, we had no real hope or confident expectation of either. Outside of Christ, hope is little more than wishful thinking. It has no grounds or assurance. It is essentially an atheistic and even godless condition. Although God had revealed Himself to us throughout creation, we refused to acknowledge Him, and instead of worshiping God, we worshiped ourselves (Rom. 1:19–25). Nothing is more hopeless than when self is sovereign. Have we forgotten that such we were?

In short, we were once "afar off." This is the summation of our existence outside of Christ. God was not near to us. Spiritually, we lived in a far country, far from God. The idea here is that God did not know us as His people. There was no immediate relationship whereby we could call upon Him. We had no experience of the nearness of God that Israel enjoyed in the Old Testament. Moses asked, "For what great nation is there that has a god so near to it as the LORD our God is to us, whenever we call upon him?" (Deut. 4:7). The obvious answer is none. God knew the people of Israel and thus was near to them. But we knew not God and did not care to know Him. Thus, God was far off from us. Have we forgotten that such we were?

The fact that these were our realities should not be lost on us, nor should we forget. But while the Bible reminds us that this was our condition, we now have a new reality—accomplished by the blood of Christ.

No Hostility at Home

The blood of Christ gives us a home. The blood of Christ becomes the flag and color under which we stand. The blood of Christ takes those who were once strangers and makes them family. As the Bible says, we are "no longer strangers and aliens, but . . . fellow citizens with the saints and members of the household of God (Eph. 2:19). Simply put, the blood of Christ brings us near to God. As Stott reminds us:

> And this nearness to God which all Christians enjoy through Christ is a privilege we take too frequently for granted. Our God does not keep his distance or stand on his dignity, like some foreign potentate, nor does he insist on any complicated ritual or protocol. On the contrary, through Jesus Christ and by the Holy Spirit we have immediate "access" to him as our Father. We need to exhort one another to avail ourselves of this privilege.[40]

The blood of Jesus tears down the walls of hostility and brings peace and prosperity of soul. It takes a people who are not His people and makes them His people under God, indivisible. The blood of Christ, spilled at the cross, is so powerful that it destroys all the foolish, oxymoronic statements we sometimes hear: "selfish Christian"—there is no self at the cross, only Jesus; "stingy Christian"—the cross is the greatest motivation for giving there could ever be; "proud Christian"—the ground at the foot of the cross is the humblest in the history of the world; or "racist Christian"—at the cross there is no Jew or Gentile, black or white, Arab or Asian. There is only Christ and those who are washed in His blood.

In Christ, the ethnic and racial identities that separate and often become the source of animosity and even enmity lose their power to divide. The blood of Christ overcomes them. Therefore, Christians must remember that there is only one family of God. We not only fly the same flag and fight under the same banner, but we share the same blood. That blood has brought us near—to God and each other. Racial and ethnic bloodlines are not omnipotent. The blood of Christ is.

When the blood of Christ brings us near, it brings us to the cross and asks us this question: "Do you remember?" Let us remember that the blood of Christ has reconciled us to God, ended the hostility, and transformed us from enemies to friends. Let us remember to pray as the songwriter suggests:

Lest I forget Gethsemane,
Lest I forget thine agony,
Lest I forget thy love for me,
Lead me to Calvary.[41]

Seven

PEACE
BY THE BLOOD

Redeemed, restored, forgiven,
Through Jesus' precious blood,
Heirs of His home in heaven,
Oh, praise our pardoning God![42]
— HENRY W. BAKER

In April 1992, after four Los Angeles Police officers were acquitted of any criminal act in the apprehension, beating, and arrest of Rodney King, the city of Los Angeles burst into one of the most bitter riots in its history. After three days of fatalities, injuries, looting, and vandalism, King appeared before the media's microphones and cameras, and asked the now-famous question: "Can't we all get along?" It seems an innocuous question, the kind I have asked my children a time or two. Yet, in the midst of race and class riots in the streets, it was a profound question about peace and tolerance.

"Can't we all get along?" is a question the religious world is fond of asking. The vast majority of those in the religious world want us to think that all beliefs and assertions of truth are equally true and valid for the purposes of knowing God and loving our fellow human beings—no matter how contradictory these beliefs and convictions may be. The religious world, which is awash in ecumenism, believes this is the way to peace. In a world of religious pluralism, the religious world's answer to King's question is, "Yes, Mr. King, we *can* all get along—if we will only live and let live, for peace comes only by accepting every opinion as equally valid, no matter how contradictory or divergent these opinions may be."

The Bible reminds us that as Christians, we are to be at peace with all people, if possible (Rom. 12:18). We are to be people who are easy to get along with, pursuers of peace and equanimity with our neighbors. Christians should not be known for violence or hate-mongering; rather, we are to be peacemakers (Matt. 5:9). Nevertheless, this peace is not to be had at the expense of the truth. In fact, the Christian knows that there is no real peace without truth, and the truth is that real, lasting peace comes only by and through the blood of Jesus.

In Colossians 1:19–20, we are told that God revealed Himself in Christ so that He might "reconcile to himself all things, whether on earth or in heaven, *making peace by the blood of his cross*" (emphasis added). This reconciliation—which brings all things into true unity and says, "Yes, we *can* get along"—comes by way of the blood of Jesus shed on the cross. However, the blood of Christ says not only that we can get along with each other; more important, it says we can get along with God.

Searching for Lost Peace

Our world is fond of talking about peace. We hold peace summits and rallies. We establish peace accords and treaties. We even hand out peace prizes. Since 1901, the Nobel Peace Prize has been awarded to a long list of distinguished recipients, such as Theodore Roosevelt, Albert Schweitzer, the Red Cross, Desmond Tutu, Mother Teresa, and Barack Obama, to name a few. Yet, for all of its summits, accords, and Nobel Prizes, the world has not achieved peace. Wars and rumors of wars continue. This is because there is no peace so long as sin remains.

Peace is the absence of hostility and the establishment of prosperity and tranquility. It is what the Bible calls *"shalom"* — a wholeness and integrity of life that is established in a right relationship with God and others. According to Eugene Peterson:

> *Shalom*, peace, is one of the richest words in the Bible. You can no more define it by looking up its meaning in the dictionary than you can define a person by his social security number. It gathers all aspects of wholeness that result from God's will being completed in us. It is the work of God that, when complete, releases streams of living water in us and pulsates with eternal life. Every time Jesus healed, forgave, or called someone, we have a demonstration of *shalom*.[43]

This *shalom* or peace reigned in the garden of Eden, but it was lost because of sin. The creation account in Genesis reminds us that God created a world established in peace. Eden was a garden of *shalom*. Out of the chaos of nothingness, God brought forth an ordered world marked by harmony, tranquility, equity, and prosperity. As the Scriptures remind us, "God saw everything that he had made, and behold, it was very good" (Gen. 1:31a). This benediction of God upon His creation was the pronouncement that all was well and at peace. Consequently, when God concluded the work of creation, the Bible says He rested on and the blessed the seventh day, sanctifying it as a day of rest and peace (2:2–3). According to one author, this rest was befitting the Creator God:

> No wonder creation culminates in the peace and joy of the Sabbath (Gen. 2:1–4a). . . . No wonder our most familiar Sabbath blessing ends: "The LORD lift up his countenance upon and give you peace [*shalom*]" (Num. 6:26), for the benediction is the affirmation of Sabbath, the conclusion of creation, when harmony has been brought to all the warring elements in our existence.[44]

In the creation, Adam and Eve existed in tranquility and prosperity with the world around them. They were at peace with the animals. They were at peace with the elements. They were at peace with each other. Most important, they were at peace with God. This peace, however, was shattered by sin. The fracturing nature of sin was manifested in the animosity and hostility that developed between humanity and the rest of creation. Because of sin, Adam and Eve were no longer at peace with nature or with each other. Because of sin, Eve would experience suffering and pain in childbirth, and Adam would experience callous-creating and often mind-numbing frustration in laboring to earn a living for himself and his family. Furthermore, the tranquility of their marital relationship was broken. The once loving, mutually prosperous relationship would now be marked by selfish, sinful desires and ambitions (Gen. 3:16–19).

Because of sin, peace in the world was broken. Worst of all, because of sin, peace with God was no more. In speaking of this fractured peace and resulting enmity, Wilhelmus à Brakel wrote:

> Due to sin there was enmity between God and man (Rom. 5:10). Sin made a separation between them both, causing God to hide His countenance from man (Is. 59:2). God hates the sinner and abhors him (Psa. 5:5–6); the face of the Lord is against him (Psa. 34:16), and His wrath is ready to destroy him (Rom. 2:5–6, 9). Conversely, man from his side has no desire after God (Job 21:14), does not delight in Him (Job 34:9), and hates God (Rom. 1:30). "The carnal mind is enmity against God" (Rom. 8:7).[45]

The loss of peace created hostility. This hostility is never more acute than in our dealings with God. In fact, while we may be able to find some measure of peace within our earthly relationships and are able to train some animals to live in harmony with us, there can be no peace with God until He declares it to be so.

Thankfully, God has come into the world and, through the blood of Christ, brought us a peace offering. He holds out to us an olive branch whereby we are able to be reconciled with Him and thus with the world. The olive branch is actually much more than a branch—it is a "tree" upon which Christ shed His blood and died. Through the blood of the cross of Christ, God has brought peace and reconciliation between our world and us, and most important, between God and us. World peace is through the blood. Alan Stibbs has correctly written:

> How then has He [Jesus] done this? Paul says first not only "through his blood" but "through the blood of his cross"; and he makes his meaning doubly and unmistakably plain by adding "in the body of his flesh through death" [Col. 1:22]. There were in Colossae Gnostic tendencies to despise things earthly, fleshly and material, and to believe that the holy things of God and much more His personal appearing and activity, could not be fully of or in this world. Paul's answer to such heresy was direct and emphatic. He declares that the universal reconciliation has been effected through something done in history, in a human body of flesh and on a cross of shame; and it was done through physical dying. So "the blood of the cross" can mean no other than the pouring out in death of His earthly life by crucifixion on a common gibbet. That is the deed that avails to put men right with God.[46]

The Promised Prince of Peace

The Old Testament promised that the Messiah would be called "Wonderful Counselor, Mighty God, Everlasting Father, Prince of Peace" (Isa. 9:6b). As Christ came to bring an end to our sin (1 John 3:5), so He came to bring peace. When Christ was born, He came as God to "give light to those who sit in darkness and in the shadow of death, to guide our feet into the way of peace" (Luke 1:79). On the night of our Savior's birth, the angels proclaimed, "Glory to God in the highest, and on earth peace among those with whom he is pleased" (Luke 2:14). Yet, the peace was not without a cost. Christ brought peace to us, but at the price of His own blood (Col. 1:20).

By His blood, Christ has not only redeemed us and forgiven us, He has also reconciled us, even restored us, to God. As the songwriter says:

> *Redeemed, restored, forgiven,*
> *Through Jesus' precious blood,*
> *Heirs of His home in heaven,*
> *Oh, praise our pardoning God!*[47]

Peace is established once again in Christ Jesus through His blood. The only way to bring an end to hostility and enmity in the world is to bring an end to the source of hostility and enmity, namely, sin—and Christ has done so.

Unfortunately, the peace of Christ is not received by everyone.

For some, Christ has brought peace. For others, He has brought a sword: "Do not think that I have come to bring peace to the earth. I have not come to bring peace, but a sword" (Matt. 10:34). Jesus Christ was not naïve. He knew the message of peace, through His life, death, and resurrection, would not be universally received. In fact, He knew it would often be viciously and violently resisted. The resistance would result in His death, and the deaths of many of those who would follow Him. Christ brings peace, but not neutrality. Those who refuse to receive the peace of Christ will find themselves at war with Christ (Luke 11:23). Consequently, for Christians, peace with Christ may also mean hostility with those who refuse to trust Him. Indeed, Jesus declared that for His sake, families would be divided, father against son, mother against daughter, and even in-laws at odds (Matt. 10:36).

Nevertheless, Christ shed His blood as the ultimate sacrifice of God to reconcile sinners to Himself. It was the ultimate gesture of amity. Those who refuse to receive the sacrifice of His blood cannot have peace with God and will often find themselves at odds with those who have. Yet, the gracious offer of peace is made to all.

We Get Along by His Blood

Why does the blood of Christ make peace? It is because without it there is no forgiveness of sin. Without the forgiveness of sin, hostility and enmity remain. Sin broke the peace in the garden of Eden, created enmity, and brought the wrath of God. As the Bible says, "The wrath of God is revealed from heaven against all ungodliness and unrighteousness of men" (Rom. 1:18a). Everyone admits there is something wrong with the world. The difference between the church and the world is not that one wants peace and the other does not. We all desire peace. The difference is that the church wants the One who has brought peace through His blood and the world does not. The difference is the blood of Jesus, which cleanses us from sin and establishes our peace with God.

> *My numerous sins transferr'd to him,*
> *Shall never more be found,*
> *Lost in his blood's atoning stream,*
> *Where every crime is drown'd!*[48]

Because of the blood of Christ, sin is no longer a barrier to a relationship with God. Yet our reconciliation with God is but a harbinger for the reconciliation that is taking place and will continue to take place throughout all creation. In the new creation, all things will be new because all things will be at peace. In the new creation, we all, once again, will get along. The blood of Christ has guaranteed it.

The world around us echoes the words of Rodney King every day: "Can't we all get along?" The church's answer to this question is the gospel of peace. We can get along in and through Jesus Christ, who by His blood is our peace and provides for us the only way to get along with God and each other.

Eight

CLEANSED BY THE BLOOD

Have you been to Jesus for His cleansing power?
Are you washed in the blood of the Lamb?
Are you fully trusting in His grace this hour?
Are you washed in the blood of the Lamb?[49]
—ELISHA A. HOFFMAN

I had some dental work done recently. Thankfully, I had a good dentist who did his best to make the experience as stress-free as possible. While I did not relish the idea of having to undergo a procedure on my tooth, today I am more than thankful for it.

But the process was not just medically helpful; it was also educational. I learned how long doctors and nurses, especially dentists, are supposed to wash their hands before and after surgery. A minimum of three minutes of scrubbing is required. I don't think I have ever washed my hands for three minutes. In fact, when I'm hungry and dinner is on the table, three seconds usually suffices. However, it was comforting to know that those who would be touching the inside of my mouth were willing to take the time to wash and scrub thoroughly.

Yet all the scrubbing and washing raised a question for me. If we can understand the need for cleanliness among doctors, how much more must cleanliness be the rule among those who would serve the holy God?

Thankfully, such cleanliness is possible. The Word of God reminds us that one of the gracious blessings of the blood of Christ is that it cleanses our consciences. The washing of our consciences creates clean hands, with which we are able to serve and worship the living God. According to Hebrews 9:13–14:

> For if the blood of goats and bulls, and the sprinkling of defiled persons with the ashes of a heifer, sanctify for the purification of the flesh, how much more will the blood of Christ, who through the eternal Spirit offered himself without blemish to God, purify our conscience from dead works to serve the living God.

The Need for Cleansing

When Adam and Eve fell into sin, they fell into a state of uncleanness. They not only fell into this state, they also plunged all of the world, and particularly humanity, into uncleanness with them. As far as God was concerned, humanity was defiled, unholy, and unclean. Sin is defiling. We must never forget this.

The tragedy of sin is not just that it kills, but that it defiles, it violates, and it dirties our consciences, our hands, and our lives beyond our ability to clean them.

Yet, no matter how dirty or defiled humanity is, no matter how destructive sin is, the one thing that sin cannot destroy is the need and desire for human beings to worship. God created us to worship. Specifically, He created us to know Him and to worship Him. Though sin distorts and misdirects this God-given impulse, it is still there.

God knows this. For this reason, when He made plans to draw His people to Himself, He provided a way for them to be cleansed so that they could worship Him. Thus, the human need for cleansing grew out of the need for worship.

If you think about it long enough, you will see the inevitable dilemma. God is holy, perfect, undefiled, and blameless. Humanity is unholy, imperfect, defiled, and guilty. How shall the unholy come to the holy? How shall the imperfect have fellowship with the perfect? How shall the defiled have an intimate relationship with the undefiled?

In the Old Testament, the answer that was given was the blood of bulls and goats. Yet, the New Testament reveals that the sacrifices of bulls and goats in the Old Testament were just stand-ins until the sacrificial blood of Jesus Christ came.

The Work of Christ

When Christ came, He put an end to the Old Testament priesthood and all of the ritual sacrifices and washings. He did this by becoming not only the Great High Priest, but also the sacrifice that washes His people from all their guilt and sin. There was a cleansing that took place in the Old Testament by the work of the priests, by way of the blood of bulls and goats. The Bible says that the work of Christ is "much more" (v. 14).

The blood of Jesus is much more than the blood of bulls and goats because it is a "once for all" sacrifice (v. 12). Unlike the sacrifices of bulls and goats in the Old Testament, the blood of Jesus was final. In the Old Testament, one year's sacrifice was not sufficient for the next. The sins of each year required a unique sacrifice and remission. However, Christ shed His blood once and for all. I like to remind my children of that which my mother always reminded me: "If you do it right the first time, you won't have to do it again." The work of Christ in securing our cleansing from all our sin was done only once because it was done right.

The text says that Christ, through His blood, purified our consciences. The conscience is the place of reality where the truth is told. It is the place out of which guilt arises, where condemnation and liberty fight for the life of a person. We ask such questions as "Does your conscience condemn you?" seeking to free people to make decisions. Or we say things like "I have a clear conscience on the matter," meaning that we do not feel that what we did was wrong. We all seek clear consciences, but the Bible reminds us that we must not only have *clear* consciences (Acts 24:16; Heb. 13:18) but also *clean* consciences (Heb. 10:22)—consciences purged from dead deeds so that we might love and worship the living God. Thus, the washing and scrubbing of hands for three minutes or three hours is not paramount, but the washing of the conscience from sin and guilt is. This comes only by the blood of Jesus. The blood of Jesus gives us what we most desperately need, namely, clean consciences. A clean conscience is representative of a clean heart. And good and God-pleasing works proceed from clean hearts. Consequently, the words of our mouths, the works of our hands, and the meditations of our hearts are acceptable in God's sight (Ps. 19:14) because they have been washed in the blood of Christ. Because our hearts have been changed, we are now able to offer service to God with clean hands.

Clean Hands

In Psalm 24, the question is raised: "Who shall ascend the hill of the LORD? And who shall stand in his holy place? He who has clean hands and a pure heart" (vv. 3–4a). The requirement for ascending to the place of God in worship is that our hands are clean and our hearts purified. The question then becomes, "Who has clean hands and a pure heart?" Whose worship in thought, word, and deed does God find fully acceptable? Whose service is perfectly pleasing to God? The only One who has such hands and such a heart is Jesus our Lord. Appropriately, the Bible reminds us that He has ascended the holy hill. He has entered the holy place, not by the temporary washing of the blood of goats and calves (Heb. 9:12), but by His own blood. By entering in, He has made a way for you and me to enter in as well (Heb. 10:19).

Does Jesus have clean hands? Yes, and so do all who have been washed in His blood. Is Jesus of a pure heart? Yes, and so are those who have been scrubbed by His blood. Through the blood of Christ, our hands and hearts have been cleared and cleansed. This means that, because of the blood of Christ, we are able to serve and worship God.

When Jesus freed the woman caught in adultery, He asked her: "Woman, where are they? Has no one condemned you?" She replied, "No one, Lord." Jesus then said to her, "Neither do I condemn you; go, and from now on sin no more" (John 8:10–11). When God has freed our consciences, it does not matter how others try to bind them. When Christ has washed our hands and hearts, it does not matter what other people say about them. We only must make sure that Christ has freed us, and that our consciences, hands, and hearts have indeed been washed in His blood.

Nevertheless, we must remember that we do not cleanse our own consciences, hands, and hearts. This was the arrogance and condemnation of Pontius Pilate. He tried to wash his hands of the guilt of Christ. The Bible says, "So when Pilate saw that he was gaining nothing, but rather that a riot was beginning, he took water and washed his hands before the crowd, saying, 'I am innocent of this man's blood'" (Matt. 27:24). While the dirt may have been removed from his hands, his conscience could not be cleansed with water. Ironically, the blood that he tried to wash away was the only blood that could have made him clean. Contrast that with Paul, who said that he served and worshiped God with a "clear conscience" (2 Tim. 1:3). The difference is that Pilate proposed to wash the blood of Christ *away* from himself, while Paul knew himself to be washed *in* the blood of Christ.

From what does the blood of Christ cleanse us? It cleanses

us from sin. Specifically, it cleans us from the sin of dead works. Hebrews 6:1 says that we need to repent of dead works. The blood of Christ cleanses us from such deeds.

Cleansed from Dead Works

Dead works are the works of our hands. These are works of self-righteousness, and they are appropriately called "dead" works because they lead to death. Twice the book of Proverbs says, "There is a way that seems right to a man, but its end is the way to death" (14:12; 16:25). We rely on work. We get significance from our work. We like a job that is well done. And well we should, because God created us to work. Yet all of our labors are useless, and thus dead, if they do not point to the worship of God. Any significance and esteem we attain from our labor apart from the end of bringing God glory and establishing His rule upon the earth is misplaced. Such godless labor may appear good to us and even receive the applause of others, but heaven finds it repulsive and defiled by sin. In other words, unless we have been washed in the blood of Christ, all our good deeds are worthless, useless, vain, and dead.

These works are lethal because the thing that most keeps people from Christ is the belief that they can be good without Him. Their lives may be filled with good deeds in the eyes of men, but such works are not necessarily good in the eyes of God. Unfortunately, many have been led astray by the church, as preachers and teachers have told them that the gospel is what they do. Live right. Eat right. Give right. Die right. The truth, however, is that only faith in Christ matters—everything else is sin (Rom. 14:23). You can sing like Mahalia Jackson or Whitney Houston. You can play like Mozart or Yo-Yo Ma. Without Christ, these works are dead. The French philosopher Blaise Pascal is believed to have said, "There are only two kinds of people in the world: the righteous who understand themselves to be sinners, and the sinners who believe themselves to be righteous." The Bible says that, apart from God in Christ, all my righteousness is but filthy rags—defiled and unclean (Isa. 64:6). Apart from the blood of Christ, my conscience and my hands are unclean, and my worship and works are dead. But in Christ, not only am I made alive, so are my works.

Worship the Living God

Why don't dead works cut it? Simply put, our God is a living God. God is not into dead things. Death and Christ are not friends. Whenever Jesus came upon a death, He reversed it. When Jesus went to a funeral, it did not stay a funeral. The Bible records three instances during the life of Jesus when He came in contact with the dead. Each time, the dead were brought back to life. He raised the son of a widow (Luke 7:11–17). He raised Jairus' daughter (Luke 8:41–42; 49–56). He raised His friend Lazarus (John 11:1–44). When Jesus touches the dead, He makes them alive. Why? Because He is alive! Consequently, to serve and worship God is to serve and worship the *living* God. Dead people do not worship a living God. This is why the Bible says we have been made alive in Christ (Eph. 2:5). We do not glory in our dead deeds. We glory in the living Christ! Only Jesus provides the clean consciences, hands, and hearts we need to glory in Him.

If the blood of Christ is required for us to have clear and clean consciences, hands, and hearts, the questions for you and me are simple, even poetic:

Have you been to Jesus for His cleansing power?
Are you washed in the blood of the Lamb?
Are you fully trusting in His grace this hour?
Are you washed in the blood of the Lamb?[50]

Nine

SANCTIFIED
BY THE BLOOD

Dear dying Lamb, Thy precious blood
Shall never lose its power,
Till all the ransomed church of God
Be saved, to sin no more.[51]
— WILLIAM COWPER

The story is told that Augustine, the fourth-century theologian and bishop of Hippo in North Africa, after confessing faith in Jesus Christ, ran into a former mistress on the street. Immediately upon recognizing her, Augustine reversed his course and began moving swiftly in the opposite direction. The woman, surprised at seeing Augustine and equally surprised at the reversal of his route, cried out, "Augustine, it is I." Augustine, continuing to move away from her, replied, "Yes, but it is not I."

This anecdote reminds us that if we are in Christ, we are

new creations. The former has passed away. The new has come (2 Cor. 5:17). In other words, Christians are changed people. The gospel and the Word of God change us. The Spirit of God changes us. The blood of Christ changes us.

This change is the manifestation of receiving new hearts and minds that have been set on fire by God. It is the result of coming to see the awfulness of our sin and the beauty, hope, and love in Jesus Christ. It is the everyday and everyway movement of our lives away from sin, Satan, and this world toward the light and glory of God in Christ Jesus. It is having our minds renewed (Rom. 12:2) even as we are being conformed to the image of Christ (8:29). It is being set apart or made holy by and for God.

This process is commonly known as sanctification. The Bible says sanctification is for the elect through the blood of Christ. According to Hebrews 13:12, "So Jesus also suffered outside the gate in order to sanctify the people through his own blood."

The Holiness of God

The Greek word for "to sanctify" is *hagiazo*. It means to be cleaned from sin or defilement and to be set apart for holy or even divine use. The related Greek word *hagios* is translated as "holy." So, when we say the blood of Christ sanctifies us, we are saying that it makes us holy. It does so because Christ is holy (1 Peter 3:15).

Putting it another way, Jesus' blood is the agent by which we are made like unto God, for God is holy. When the angels in heaven give us a description of the sovereign God they worship, they call out, "Holy, holy, holy is the LORD of hosts; the whole earth is full of his glory!" (Isa. 6:3). The angels do not call God just "holy." They call Him "holy, holy, holy." In his classic work *The Holiness of God*, R. C. Sproul explains:

> Only once in sacred Scripture is an attribute of God elevated to the third degree. Only once is a characteristic of God mentioned three times in succession. The Bible says that God is holy, holy, holy. Not that He is merely holy, or even holy, holy. He is holy, holy, holy. The Bible never says that God is love, love, love; or mercy, mercy, mercy; or wrath, wrath, wrath; or justice, justice, justice. It does say that He is holy, holy, holy, that the whole earth is full of His glory.[52]

God is holy. This means He is separate from sin. His holiness is such that He cannot have sin in His presence or be in loving fellowship with anything touched by it. Thus, for God to have fellowship with us, we must be sanctified, that is, made clean from sin. This is the work of the blood of Christ. If the sacrifices in the Old Testament made the Israelites momentarily acceptable in God's sight, how much more does the superior, all-sufficient, once-and-for-all sacrifice of Christ on the cross make us eternally acceptable in God's sight (Heb. 9:13; 10:10).

This is important for us to understand because it reminds us that sanctification is first outside of us. It is what Christ accomplished for us. He is made for us "wisdom from God, righteousness and sanctification" (1 Cor. 1:30). This sanctification is the work of His blood for us. As Stephen Charnock reminds us:

There is a cleansing from guilt, and a cleansing from filth; both are the fruits of this blood: the guilt is removed by remission, the filth by purification. Christ does both: he cleanses us from our guilt as he is our righteousness, from our spot as he is our sanctification; for he is both to us (1 Cor. 1:30).[53]

All those who have come to Jesus by faith and have trusted in His death on the cross as the basis for the forgiveness of their sin are saved and sanctified. In other words, in heaven we are holy. Our everyday lives are but the practical living out of that which is our eternal and ethereal reality positionally. The blood of Christ has changed our standing before the sight of God. Our lives should demonstrate this glorious change before the sight of men.

"I Ain't What I Was"

"Are you saved, sanctified, and filled with the Holy Ghost; speaking in tongues as the Spirit gives you utterance?" That question was posed to me when I worshiped with a friend who attended a "Pentecostal Holiness" church.

When many people think of sanctification or holiness, they often think of a certain kind of Christian. They may think of the storefront "holiness" church or the long-dressed, hat-wearing "sanctified" lady. Unfortunately, too many perceive sanctification as the young man who lives by this axiom:

Don't smoke,
Don't chew,

And don't go out with girls who do.
Don't play cards
Or games of chance,
Or hang around with boys who dance.

These emphases have led many people to believe that "holy" is a separate designation for a certain class of Christian. They think sanctification is for those who have been able to achieve an uncommon separateness from this world or have received "the baptism of the Spirit" or a "second blessing" that is evidenced by speaking in tongues. Therefore, sanctification is not something everyone can accomplish.

However, the Bible speaks of sanctification as belonging to all who have trusted Christ. If you have come to Jesus Christ by faith, Jesus has sanctified you. His blood has made you holy, righteous, and set apart unto Him. Your heart, mind, and body have been set apart for Christ. This is the truth over which heaven rejoices for you.

However, not only does heaven rejoice, but those on earth take notice, too, not because you speak in other tongues but because you control the tongue with which you speak everyday. So radical is the sanctifying blood of Christ that it eventually and necessarily begins to show in your life. People notice that you are different. You notice that you are different. There is a movement in your heart away from the desires of this world toward a growing desire for Christ. It is not going out of the world altogether, but it is a desire to be distinct from the world while seeking to influence and serve the world. J. I. Packer reminds us:

The Christian's holiness, like his Master's, is his living out a relationship to the world of men where he is in it without being of it (see John 17:14–16). This requires both separation and identification, both detachment and involvement.[54]

For example, when the Christians in Corinth were struggling to understand the difference Christ had made in them, the Apostle Paul gave a laundry list of sinful behaviors and reminded the Corinthians that the unregenerate, the unchanged, and those unmoved by the gospel would not inherit the kingdom of God (1 Cor. 6:9–10). But then he said: "And such *were* some of you. But you were washed, you *were sanctified*, you were justified in the name of the Lord Jesus Christ and by the Spirit of our God" (v. 11, emphasis added). He told them that their lives were to be morally distinct from the world, and yet they were not to understand him as calling them away from any contact with the world (5:10). The sanctifying blood of Christ makes a difference in our living in the presence of this world day to day.

So, the sanctifying blood of Christ makes all the difference in our being in the presence of God for eternity. The blood of Christ has secured our holiness in the sight of God. Because the blood of Christ has been shed for us, our position in the eyes of God is secure. We are in Christ, and we are holy as He is holy. Nevertheless, Christ is doing an ongoing work of making us practically what we have become positionally, namely, holy.

There are times in our lives when we do not feel the ongoing, progressive nature of our sanctification. We may even get the sense that rather than progressing, we are regressing due to our perpetual struggle with indwelling sin. It is during such times that the gospel reminds us that our sanctification does not happen because we are willing to shed our blood but because Christ was willing to shed His. It is not our blood and sacrifice that has pleased the Father; it is the blood of His beloved Son. Thus, when the battle for daily holiness appears lost, encourage yourself with the words of the old saints: "I ain't what I wanna be; I ain't what I'm gonna be; but through the blood of Christ, I ain't what I was."

From Self to Satan

The path to sanctification in this life is wrought with needful and important conversations. There is the internal conversation we have with ourselves, reminding ourselves to be patient with our sanctification because God is not finished with us yet. The ongoing work of sanctifying grace is just that—ongoing. Yet, at times, we also need to have conversations with our Enemy. Satan knows our weaknesses, and he often sees when we fail. He is quick to remind us of our lack of progress in the gospel and how often we appear to fall short in our conformity to Christ.

In John Bunyan's classic *The Pilgrim's Progress*, Christian is making his way along life's path to the Celestial City. Along the way, he meets Apollyon, who is Bunyan's depiction of Satan. Apollyon is quick to lay upon Christian the guilt of his failures and the seeming lack of progress Christian is making in his journey of faith. Seeking to discourage Christian, Apollyon reminds him of his unfaithfulness to Christ:

Apollyon: Thou hast already been unfaithful in thy service to Him; how dost thou think to receive wages of Him?

Christian: Wherein, O Apollyon, have I been unfaithful to Him?

Apollyon: Thou didst faint at first setting out, when thou wast almost choaked in the Gulph of Despond; thou didst attempt wrong ways to be rid of thy burden, whereas thou shouldst have stayed till thy Prince had taken it off. Thou didst sinfully sleep, and lose thy choice things. Thou wast also almost persuaded to go back at the sight of the lions: and when thou talkest of thy journey, and of what thou hast heard and seen, thou art inwardly desirous of vain-glory in all that thou sayest and dost.

Christian: All this is true, and much more, which thou has left out; but the Prince whom I serve and honour is merciful and ready to forgive: but besides, these infirmities possessed me in thy Country; for there I sucked them in, and I have groaned under them, been sorry for them, and have obtained pardon of my Prince.[55]

The Bible reminds us that Satan is not only the tempter, but he is also the accuser (Rev. 12:10). If he cannot get us to denounce our confession of faith, he seeks to accuse us of failing to live consistently in accordance with our faith. Like Apollyon, he works to remind us of our struggle with sin. When this is the case, consider the words of Charitie L. Bancroft:

When Satan tempts me to despair
And tells me of the guilt within,
Upward I look and see Him there
Who made an end of all my sin.
Because the sinless Savior died
My sinful soul is counted free,
For God, the Just, is satisfied
To look on Him and pardon me.[56]

Jesus made an end to all our sin by suffering as our sin offering outside the gate (Lev. 4:21; Heb. 13:12). By doing this, He not only sanctified us, but He made the way for our growth in sanctification in this life.

The blood of Jesus has laid the path of holiness. Though the pace of our steps along the path is often varied, the path yet endures. So, keep moving, Christian. The Bible reminds us "what we will be has not yet appeared; but we know that when he appears we shall be like him, because we shall see him as he is" (1 John 3:2). In other words, keep moving. Keep marching. God is not through with us yet.

Ten
—

ELECT
IN THE BLOOD

And can it be that I should gain
An interest in the Savior's blood?
Died He for me, who caused His pain—
For me, who Him to death pursued?[57]
— CHARLES WESLEY

The first presidential election in America took place in 1788–89. The polls opened on December 15, 1788, and closed on January 10, 1789. In this election, George Washington was chosen as the first president of the United States. Arguably the most popular president in American history, Washington remains the only president ever elected with one hundred percent of the Electoral College. Thus, the process of electing presidents was established in America.

For many, the ballot box is what makes America a great

place. We elect our officials. To be chosen by the people for such an honor as the presidency should be a humbling experience. If this is true in regard to an election by people, how much more should it be true in regard to an election by God? Just as the people make their choice in an election, the Bible says God's act of choosing is "election."

This election, according to Peter, is for the sprinkling of sinners with Christ's blood. He refers to Christians as "those who are elect . . . according to the foreknowledge of God the Father, in the sanctification of the Spirit, for obedience to Jesus Christ and *for the sprinkling with his blood*" (1 Peter 1:1–2, emphasis added). Here we see that God's chosen people are known by the Father, are the recipients of the Spirit's sanctifying work, and are redeemed through the blood of the Son, Jesus Christ.

However, while we elect our representatives based on the potential for good in them, God's election is based solely on His good and sovereign pleasure. Here is a good, succinct definition of the doctrine of election: "Election is an act of God before the creation in which He chooses some people to be saved, not on account of any foreseen merit in them, but only because of his sovereign, good pleasure"[58] (Rom. 9:11; Eph. 1:4).

The Sovereign, Gracious, Loving Choice of God

To understand election is to see it as the act of a sovereign, gracious, eternally loving God. It is a demonstration of His desire to be in a faithful covenantal relationship with a people. Though knowing these people to be disobedient, sinful, and wayward, He chooses to set His affection on them so as to show and exalt His love and mercy throughout eternity. Consequently, divine election has three important elements:

Election is unconditional. God did not choose His people based on who we are or what we can do, on any potential we have or that He saw in us. Rather, He chose us when we had met no prior condition or obligation. To illustrate this incomparable truth, the Bible uses the story of twins Jacob and Esau:

> When Rebekah had conceived children by one man, our forefather Isaac, though they were not yet born and had done nothing either good or bad—in order that God's purpose of election might continue, not because of works but because of him who calls—she was told, "The older will serve the younger." As it is written, "Jacob I loved, but Esau I hated." (Rom. 9:10–13)

We elect presidents based on what we hear and see. We choose spouses based on the impression they make upon us. But God's choice of His beloved was not based on any goodness in them. He made His choice without respect of person. As one Puritan writer put it, "Moreover, as God respects no persons, so He respects no condition upon which He gives salvation to us.[59]

Election is eternal. God's choices are as old as He is. When did God choose you? When you were born? When you believed? No. He chose you from all eternity. The electing purpose of God is from before the beginning and will be true throughout all eternity. A lady once told John Newton, "If God had not chosen me before I was born, he would have never chosen me afterwards."[60] The Bible speaks of God as the One "who saved us and called us to a holy calling, not because of our works but because of his own purpose and grace, which he gave us in Christ Jesus before the ages began" (2 Tim. 1:9).

Election is loving. Some people think the biblical doctrine of election is unloving. They suggest that because God has not chosen everyone for salvation, only some, then He is not loving. Yet, the very opposite is true. Because God loves, He chooses. Love by nature must be particular, specifically designed for a beloved. To love all the same without discrimination or distinction is to not love at all.

Practically speaking, we understand this. Would my wife think me more loving if I loved all women the same way I love her? Or would she desire my love for her to be distinguished from the love I have for others? Would she consider me unloving if I told her I loved only her? The answers are obvious. God's love is an electing love, and His election is a loving election. Love is the key! In choosing or electing the Israelites to be His people from among all the other people in the world, God declared:

> "For you are a people holy to the LORD your God. The LORD your God has chosen you to be a people for his treasured possession, out of all the peoples who are on the face of the earth. It was not because you were more in number than any other people that the LORD set his love on you and chose you, for you were the fewest of all peoples, but it is because the LORD loves you and is

keeping the oath he swore to your fathers, that the LORD has brought you out with a mighty hand and redeemed you from the house of slavery, from the hand of Pharaoh king of Egypt." (Deut. 7:6–8)

"Elect" is a term of loving endearment. In the Bible, particularly the New Testament, God's people are consistently referred to as the "elect" or the "chosen" (Rom. 8:33; Col. 3:12; 1 Thess. 1:4; 2 Tim. 2:10; 1 Peter 2:9). In fact, this is one of the favorite ways in which the New Testament writers are moved to refer to God's people.

Peter specifically reminds us that election is the loving purpose of God. He writes his epistle more to console than to correct, comforting his readers in their distresses by first reminding them that they are chosen by God.

He also tells them how and why they have been chosen. It is the work of a triune God. They are elect according to the Father's foreknowledge, in the Spirit's sanctification, and for obedience to the Son, Jesus Christ. All this is realized through the blood of Christ (1 Peter 1:1–2).

The Foreknowledge of God the Father

The idea of God's foreknowledge is not just that God knows of us before we know of Him (Ps. 139); it is also that what God foreknows, He foreordains. Romans 8:29 reminds us that those whom God foreknows He also predestines or predetermines to be made over in the image of Christ. How can God know we will be made like Christ? He knows because He ordains that we will be so remade.

How did God know that Jesus would be born in Bethlehem? How did God know that the Jewish leaders would plot Jesus' death and that Judas would betray Him? How did God know that Jesus would be put to death on the cross, that He would be raised three days later, and that our salvation would be eternally secured? He knew it all because He ordained it all to come to pass. Peter, preaching on the day of Pentecost, put it this way:

> "Men of Israel, hear these words: Jesus of Nazareth, a man attested to you by God with mighty works and wonders and signs that God did through him in your midst, as you yourselves know—this Jesus, delivered up according to the definite plan and foreknowledge of God, you crucified and killed by the hands of lawless men. God raised him up, loosing the pangs of death, because it was not possible for him to be held by it." (Acts 2:22–24)

From the cradle to the cross to the crown, God ordained the life of Christ. His coming from glory, assuming the humility of humanity, suffering, dying, and being raised to glory again was all in accordance with the foreknowledge of God.

If you are in Christ, you, too, have been so lovingly known. When you realize that you are a foreigner or stranger in the world, it is comforting to know that you are known and loved by God. Like the people of Israel, who lived in the midst of hostile foreign nations, Christians are scattered throughout the hostile world.

Challenges to living faithfully in a faithless world are many. How do we cope? Remember, no matter where you are, God knows you. He has elected you. While you may be a stranger in this world, you are no stranger to God. You are His beloved. You are elect according to the foreknowledge of the Father.

The Sanctification of the Spirit

The Spirit of God is the Holy Spirit. Wherever He comes, He comes with holiness and sanctification. Here we see that the loving goal of our sanctification is that the Spirit will change us. God is making us new. The purpose in election is not just eternity with God in sinless bliss, but it is the everyday outworking of our salvation with the fear of God in our lives. If we are elect, it will show in our progression toward God in holiness and reverence: "he chose us in him before the foundation of the world, that we should be holy and blameless before him" (Eph. 1:4). God chose us *in* holiness and He chose us *to* holiness. Election is the love and grace of God to us. Sanctification is the Spirit of God working through us to make that election, calling, and choice sure (2 Peter 1:10).

Yet, as we all know, often before we can make something new, we have to tear down the old. As God is making us new, He is also tearing down the old, and it does not always feel good. He is giving us new minds, new affections, new priorities, even new habits of speech. As Paul says: "Therefore, if anyone is in Christ, he is a new creation. The old has passed away; behold, the new has come" (2 Cor. 5:17).

For Obedience to the Son

Joyful obedience is the only faithful response to the gospel and the right response to election. The Bible reminds us that our obedience is an obedience of faith (Rom. 1:5; 16:26). It is the necessary and faithful consequence of the love of God in choosing sinners to be saved in Christ Jesus. If we love Christ, we joyfully obey Him (John 14:15). The commands of Christ are the loving edicts of a faithful Master. Like Peter (2 Peter 1:1), Paul (Rom. 1:1; Phil. 1:1), and James (James 1:1), we have no problem in calling ourselves slaves of Christ, who alone is worthy of our loving, unquestioned obedience.

When I was a boy, I obeyed my parents because of what I thought they would do to me if I did not (as most kids do). As I have matured, so has my obedience. Today I obey my mother not because I am afraid of what she will do to me, but because now I realize all that she has done for me. This is the obedience of faith—gospel obedience. We obey God not because we are afraid of what He will do to us if we do not. Rather, we obey Him because we are moved by all that He has done for us in Jesus Christ. He has lovingly elected us and sprinkled us with the sin-forgiving, grace-abounding blood of Jesus.

For Sprinkling with His Blood

Here we see the blood of Christ confirming the covenantal work of God on behalf of His chosen people. Peter's imagery harkens back to the days when the people of Israel were gathered at Mount Sinai. Having been redeemed from their cruel bondage in Egypt by God's gracious, mighty hand, and having received God's law through Moses, the Israelites assembled to hear the Word of God proclaimed to them. The Bible says that Moses "took the Book of the Covenant and read it in the hearing of the people. And they said, 'All that the LORD has spoken we will do, and we will be obedient.' And Moses took the blood and threw it on the people and said, 'Behold the blood of the covenant that the LORD has made with you in accordance with all these words'" (Ex. 24:7–8).

The elect or chosen of God have been sprinkled with the blood of Christ unto the forgiveness of their sin and the confirmation that they are the beloved people of God. If the blood of oxen proved sufficient to confirm the election of the people of Old Testament Israel, how much more does the blood of Christ sprinkled on His New Testament church confirm its election? Contemplating the loving, electing grace of God in the blood of Christ, hymnwriter Charles Wesley raised a question we all should ponder often:

> And can it be that I should gain
> An interest in the Savior's blood?
> Died He for me, who caused His pain—
> For me, who Him to death pursued?
> Amazing love! How can it be
> That Thou, my God, shouldst die for me?[61]

God has elected a people for His own possession. Unfortunately, in our fallible system of political election, there are times when recounts and runoffs are necessary. This is not so with the Lord, however. Thankfully, His electing grace is not in accordance with the human ballot box but in accordance with His own blood.

Eleven

RANSOMED BY THE BLOOD

For nothing good have I
Whereby Thy grace to claim.
I'll wash my garments white
In the blood of Calv'ry's Lamb.[62]
—ELVINA M. HALL

The story is told that Abraham Lincoln went down to the slave block and there noticed a young black girl up for auction. Moved with compassion, he bid on her and won. Upon purchasing her, Lincoln told the disbelieving girl that she was free. In her surprise, she said, "What does that mean?"

"It means you are free," he replied.

"Does that mean," she asked, "I can say whatever I want to say?"

"Yes, my dear, you can say whatever you want to say."

"Does that mean I can be whatever I want to be?"

"Yes, you can be whatever you want to be."

"Does that mean I can go wherever I want to go?"

"Yes, you can go wherever you want to go."

At that, the girl, with tears streaming down her face, said, "Then I will go with you."

Admittedly, this account is probably more legendary than legitimate. Yet it does communicate an important spiritual truth. Like the young girl on the slave block, we, too, have been redeemed and set free. The Bible reminds us in 1 Peter 1:18–19 that if we are in Christ, we have been "ransomed from the futile ways inherited from [our] forefathers, not with perishable things such as silver or gold, but with the precious blood of Christ." The blood of Christ is of incalculable value, and for that reason it alone is able to ransom sinners from their slavery to sin.

Slavery to Sin

Before Christ, we were sold into slavery to sin. Our hearts, our souls, and our bodies were captive to it. We had no choice but to sin, for we were "slaves of sin" (Rom. 6:17). Yet unlike the slave girl, we loved our captivity and reveled in it. We lived happily in the foolishness of our minds and the bliss of our ignorance. We relished every foolish, ignorant moment. We loved the world and we hated God (Rom. 8:7). We loved the passions of our flesh and deemed God unnecessary and His Word irrelevant for daring to challenge our lives. We were lovers of self rather than lovers of God (2 Tim. 3:2–4). We were on the broad road to hell and happy to be there.

Into this situation came the Lord. He came to us while we were His enemies (Rom. 5:10). He came to us while we were in the chains of the Devil and the grip of this world. He came and set us free—free from slavery to sin, free from the chains of the Evil One, free from the grip of this world and the bondage of our fleshly lusts and desires. The Lord of heaven came to the slave block of sin, saw us in our helpless, degraded, and hopeless state, and bought us. As the Bible says, God ransomed us (1 Peter 1:18). He paid the price to free us, and now we are free.

Yet, the price was not paid with greenbacks, silver, or gold. It was not paid with any currency traded in this world, for our captivity was beyond the power of any earthly currency to affect. Our redemption required a currency traded only in heaven. We were set free with the most precious currency of all, the blood of Christ. Silver and gold are commodities for which men and women have killed and died. They are priceless in the eyes of the world. In the eyes of heaven, the blood of Christ is not just priceless, it is precious. It is of infinite worth. As the song says, "Had I the guilt of all the world, He's able to forgive."[63]

His blood has redeemed us. His blood has set us free. And like the young slave girl, we should desire nothing more than to live for and with the One who has redeemed us.

In fact, Peter reminds us that our priceless redemption should provide the motivation for loving, joyful, holy obedience to Christ: "As obedient children, do not be conformed to the passions of your former ignorance, but as he who called you is holy, you also be holy in all your conduct, since it is written, 'You shall be holy, for I am holy'" (1 Peter 1:14–16). We are called to holiness, not in order that we might be ransomed, but because we already have been so graciously ransomed.

In the Old Testament, when God redeemed the people of Israel out of Egypt, He did it through the blood of lambs upon the doorposts of their homes. Yet the end of their redemption was not just a flight out of Egypt, but also their establishment as a holy nation, a kingdom of priest set apart for God (Ex. 19:5–6). As one author states it, "They [Israel] were redeemed by blood; and redeemed not only from judgement [sic] but to be a people for the Lord's own possession."[64] Likewise, our redemption is more than just a flight out of sin and this world. Rather, we have been redeemed, not by the blood of a farm-raised lamb, but by the precious blood of the Lamb of God. Therefore, how much more are we to understand that we are, more so than Israel was, "a chosen race, a royal priesthood, a holy nation, a people for [God's] own possession" (1 Peter 2:9). This is the ground for our pursuit of holiness. This is our motivation for living as lights in this world.

Blood-Bought Motivations for Holiness

Peter gives us two truths worth remembering as motivations for our pursuit of holiness. First, we must remember from what we have been ransomed. The Bible says we have been ransomed "from the futile ways inherited from [our] forefathers" (1 Peter 1:18). Life apart from a right relationship with God is futile. "Vanity of vanities," the Bible calls it (Eccl. 1:2). No matter how religious, lavish, or popular your life before Christ was, it was empty. How empty? The Apostle Paul called it *skubalon* ("rubbish, dung, sewage"):

> For we are the circumcision, who worship by the Spirit of God and glory in Christ Jesus and put no confidence in the flesh—though I myself have reason for confidence in the flesh also. If anyone else thinks he has reason for confidence in the flesh, I have more: circumcised on the eighth day, of the people of Israel, of the tribe of Benjamin, a Hebrew of Hebrews; as to the law, a Pharisee; as to zeal, a persecutor of the church; as to righteousness under the law, blameless. But whatever gain I had, I counted as loss for the sake of Christ. Indeed, I count everything as loss because of the surpassing worth of knowing Christ Jesus my Lord. For his sake I have suffered the loss of all things and count them as rubbish, in order that I may gain Christ. (Phil. 3:3–8)

According to Paul, his life prior to Christ would have been the envy of most in his world. He had everything anyone in his world could have wanted, and most of it was inherited from his forefathers. He had social status, religious status, educational status, financial status, and moral status. He was a pillar in his society, considered righteous and blameless. Yet, upon the revelation of Jesus Christ in his life, when Jesus ransomed him, Paul came to see all these things as loss, worthless, or even refuse and rubbish. In comparison to knowing Christ, these cultural, ethnic, and social riches were worthless. They belonged to the world of waste and deserved to be disregarded and disdained as such. While his society would have counted his status worthy of envy, Paul said it was futile, a vanity of vanities. Paul was ransomed from such vain pursuits, and so are all who have been cleansed by the blood of Christ.

In Philippians 3:3–8 and 1 Peter 1:18, we see Paul and Peter saying the same thing. In Christ, we are ransomed from that futile, vain living that was ours from birth and that had been accumulating ever since. The idea of futility or worthlessness was particularly significant and poignant in Peter's world, because he was writing to people who, in most cases, like Paul, were the first Christians in their families. Undoubtedly, many came from strongly traditional Jewish homes. Yet, Peter said many of the rituals their parents had handed down to them were empty and worthless, leading to bondage and away from God. But God, through the blood of Christ, had delivered them. Likewise, He has delivered us from futile things. The greatness of this deliverance should not be forgotten. We could not know the futility of our lives until we were made to see the utility of Christ.

Second, we must remember that with which we have been ransomed. Peter says that we have been ransomed not with perishable things but with the precious blood of Christ (1 Peter 1:19). Someone has said that salvation is free. Yes, it is free in that it does not cost silver, gold, dollars, or cents. But that does not mean that it does not cost anything. In fact, it cost Christ everything. Salvation is free to you and me because someone else paid the price:

Jesus paid it all,
All to Him I owe;
Sin had left a crimson stain,
He washed it white as snow.[65]

It's one thing to ransom someone from slavery in this world. Many have performed this gracious act, and we thank God for it. But how do we ransom people from slavery to sin? How much do we pay to ransom them from death and hell? For such a transaction, silver and gold are of no value. There is an economy wherein the only currency is the blood of Christ. It is God's economy. It is the economy of the kingdom of God. It is the economy of the redeemed. To redeem us, Christ did not reach into the treasure bag; He reached into Himself—the treasure of all treasures—and set us free.

No Reserves, No Retreats, No Regrets

William Borden graduated from high school in Chicago in 1904. He was the heir of the Borden Dairy estate. For graduation, he received the uncommon gift of a trip around the world. Little did those who gave him this trip realize what it would do to him. While on the trip, William began to feel a burden for those less fortunate and those in need of Christ around the world. He wrote home expressing a desire to give his life in service to Christ as a missionary. Though friends and relatives stood in disbelief, Borden wrote two words in the back of his Bible: "No reserves."

He returned to America and enrolled at Yale University. He was a model student. Though others might have thought college life would quench William's desire for the mission field, it only fueled it. He started a Bible study, and by the end of his first year 150 students were meeting weekly to study the Scriptures and pray. By the time he was a senior, one thousand of the thirteen hundred students at Yale were in discipleship groups meeting for weekly Bible study and prayer.

He did not limit his evangelistic efforts simply to the up-and-out around Yale's pristine campus. His heart was equally for the down-and-out. He founded the Yale Hope Mission. He ministered to those who were on the streets of New Haven, Connecticut. He shared the ministry of Christ with orphans, widows, the homeless, and the hungry, offering them hope and refuge. A visitor from oversees was asked what impressed him most during his time in America. He responded, "The sight of that young millionaire kneeling with his arm around a 'bum' in the Yale Hope Mission."[66]

When Borden graduated from Yale, he was offered many lucrative jobs. Yet to the dismay of many relatives and friends, he refused. Instead, he wrote in the back of his Bible two more words: "No retreat." He entered Princeton Seminary and, upon graduation, set sail for China. Intending to serve Christ among the Muslim populations, he stopped over in Egypt to study and learn Arabic. However, while there, he contracted spinal meningitis. He lived only a month longer. At the age of twenty-five, William Borden was dead.

Borden counted all things loss for the sake of knowing Christ and making Him known. He refused to be taken in by the futility of the life inherited from his forefathers, but rather sought to live out the glory of his ransom by the blood of Jesus Christ. When his Bible was discovered after his death, it was found that he had added two more words to the back page: "No regrets."

Those who know the price of their redemption also know that a life lived for the One who ransomed them is a life with no regrets. Like the slave girl, William Borden chose to go with the One who had ransomed him. How about you?

Twelve

FREED
BY THE BLOOD

Would you be free from the burden of sin?
There's power in the blood, power in the blood.
Would you o'er evil a victory win?
There's wonderful power in the blood.[67]
—LEWIS E. JONES

S in not only contaminates, it also subjugates. That is, it
enslaves. Like a great snake—a python or anaconda—sin
wraps itself around us and slowly entangles and strangles us. The
more we struggle against it in our strength, the more we find
ourselves entangled in it. It beats us into submission, locking us
into servitude that is hard and inextricable. It is an enslaver of the
worst kind. It is no respecter of persons. The young and old, the
rich and poor alike are all under its sway.

Sin has a power unparalleled on earth. It is more destructive than an atomic bomb; more menacing than a terrorist plot; more ruinous than a plague of locusts; more devastating than ten tsunamis; and more horrible and scary than a thousand bogeymen. Those who have been caught in its grip can testify to this truth. Many have been the cries of those trapped in the darkness of sexual perversion and addiction with seemingly no way out. Even more have experienced the perpetual night of drugs and alcoholism with seemingly no light or even the promise of day. Listen to the men or women who cannot resist the latest bit of gossip. They want to stop, they want to resist, but the temptation to hear and pass on scintillating news is too strong. They are held captive by sin, and their struggles to escape appear futile.

Is there an exit? Can those trapped in the grip of sin escape? Is it possible to be set free from the power of sin? As we conclude our trek through the New Testament looking at the glories of the blood of Christ for the redeemed, we read in Revelation 1:5: "Jesus Christ [is] the faithful witness, the firstborn of the dead, and the ruler of kings on earth. [He] loves us and has freed us from our sins by his blood." Freedom from sin is possible—by Christ's blood.

Freed by Our Prophet, Priest, and King

As powerful as sin is, the blood of Christ is more powerful still. In Christ, the chains of our captivity have been broken, and the light of His grace has shone the way of freedom. But how has He freed us? Christ has secured our freedom because, in the shedding of His blood, He operated in the divinely ordained *munus triplex*, the threefold office of Prophet, Priest, and King. This is why He is called "the faithful witness" (as Prophet); "the first-born of the dead" (as Priest); and "the ruler of kings on earth" (as King). In the threefold office of Christ, we are granted our freedom from sin.

As Prophet, Jesus pronounced an end to all our sin. In the Old Testament, the prophet was the mouthpiece of God to the people. In fact, the prophet often prefaced his words by saying, "Thus says the Lord." As God's mouthpiece, the prophet spoke the words of indictment against the people for their sin (Isa. 1:4) and called them to repentance (v. 18). The prophet pronounced the forgiveness and pardon of God (Isa. 40:1–2). Jesus, as the final and sufficient Prophet, has done all of these for us. He came not just proclaiming the Word of God; He is the Word of God (John 1:1). He came to the world because of sin (Matt. 1:21). He proclaimed our need to repent and believe on Him (Mark 1:15). And He proclaimed our pardon and forgiveness for sin (Col. 1:14).

As Priest, Jesus offered Himself as the sacrifice for all our sin. In the Old Testament, the high priest was the mediator between the holy God and His sinful people. As mediator, the high priest entered the Holy Place and offered a sacrifice to God on behalf of the people once a year on the Day of Atonement (Lev. 16:34). He sprinkled the blood of the sacrifice on the mercy seat "because of the uncleanness of the people of Israel and because of their transgressions, all their sins" (Lev. 16:16). This he did year after year after year. Christ, as our Mediator and High Priest, not only *offered* the sacrifice (once and for all), but He *is* the sacrifice. Like the high priest of old, Christ entered the Holy Place, but unlike the high priest, He entered to offer Himself. He had to enter only one time, for He sprinkled His own blood on the mercy seat. As the writer of Hebrews reminds us:

> But when Christ appeared as a high priest of the good things that have come, then through the greater and more perfect tent (not made with hands, that is, not of this creation) he entered once for all into the holy places, not by means of the blood of goats and calves but by means of his own blood, thus securing an eternal redemption. For if the blood of goats and bulls, and the sprinkling of defiled persons with the ashes of a heifer, sanctify for the purification of the flesh, how much more will the blood of Christ, who through the eternal Spirit offered himself without blemish to God, purify our conscience from dead works to serve the living God. (Heb. 9:11–14)

As King, Jesus rules in such a way as not to allow sin to reign over us any longer. In the Old Testament, the monarchy was established for the peace, prosperity, and welfare of the nation. The prototype king was David. No king was ever as beloved as he was. He was God's viceregent among the people. With David on the throne, the nation of Israel could say, "All is well." Few things comfort a nation more than having a ruler of righteousness and strength sitting on the throne of power. It was said of David that he "reigned over all Israel. And David administered justice and equity to all his people" (2 Sam. 8:15). However, we have a King greater than David. Christ came in the line of David as David's son and yet also as David's Lord (Matt. 22:42–45). He is "the ruler of kings on earth" (Rev. 1:5) and "King of kings and Lord of lords" (19:16), including David. He rules with perfect justice and equity. As our King, He has fought our battles and now rules in such a way that sin never can reign over us (Rom. 6:7–14).

Freed in Love

In Christ, we have a Prophet who has brought the Word of God to us; we have a Priest who has offered Himself in our place; and we have a King who rules with justice and equity over His people. All of this is rooted in the fact that our Savior loves us. At the heart of everything Christ does for us is His love for us. This includes securing our freedom. As Revelation 1:5 reminds us, our Prophet, Priest, and King loved us enough to set us free.

We are set free by the blood of our Prophet, Priest, and King so that we, in turn, become like prophets, priests, and kings. Because we have been set free, we are like prophets who speak the truth in Christ; we do not lie (Rom. 9:1). Because we have been set free, we are a kingdom of priests (Ex. 19:6; 1 Peter 2:9), ready to offer our lives in service to God and each other, even as we intercede on behalf of earthly rulers and authorities (1 Tim. 2:1–2). Because the King has set us free, we anticipate the day when we shall reign over all along with Christ (2 Tim. 2:12).

In Christ, we are freed from sin, and now grace reigns in

righteousness (Rom. 5:21). Consequently, because we are now a royal priesthood, we live like peasants when we wallow in the sin of this world. The blood of Christ has freed us from the mire and murkiness of our sin. We are free from the tyranny of the world's standards; free from the black hole of the ungodly expectations of others; free from the guilt of all our past transgressions and infidelities; free from the world's sinful standard of what a successful woman or man is; free to be men and women of God; free to serve Christ with our whole hearts; free to be different; free to live for Jesus at every turn and at whatever cost; free to die for Jesus; and free to live again in Jesus.

It may sound unusual, and in most Christian circles it is not heard, but the biblical truth and reality is that we do not have to sin. We are no longer in bondage to sin. We do not have to give in to temptation. We can bring the flesh into subjection to the will of God. We can discipline our bodies "and keep [them] under control" (1 Cor. 9:27). We can flee from temptations (1 Cor. 6:18; 10:14; 1 Tim. 6:11; 2 Tim. 2:22). We can resist the Devil (James 4:7). These verses and others remind us that the power to not sin lies within those set free from sin by the blood of Jesus. The power of the blood does not simply free us from sin, but it also frees us unto righteousness (Rom. 6:18). Charles Spurgeon summed it up for us:

> Unspeakably precious, is his blood, because it has an overcoming power. It is written, "They overcame through the blood of the Lamb." How could they do otherwise? He who fights with the precious blood of Jesus, fights

with a weapon which cannot know defeat. The blood of Jesus! Sin dies at its presence, death ceases to be death: heaven's gates are opened. The blood of Jesus! We shall march on, conquering and to conquer; so long as we can trust its power![68]

Thirteen

HIS BLOOD AVAILS FOR YOU

He breaks the power of canceled sin,
He sets the prisoner free.
His blood can make the foulest clean,
His blood availed for me.[69]
— JOHN WESLEY

To speak of the blood of Christ is to speak of what Christ accomplished for us in pouring out His life unto death. Our salvation was accomplished by Christ "becoming obedient to the point of death, even death on a cross" (Phil. 2:8). On the cross, He shed His blood for us. On the cross, He gave His life for us. The blood that Jesus shed on the cross was enough to appease the righteous wrath of God against our sin. It was enough to reconcile us to God. It was enough to cleanse us from the sin inherited from Adam and the sin we actively commit every day.

It was sufficient for God to declare us free and in a right relationship with Him.

But how do we *know* the blood of Jesus was enough? How do we *know* that the sacrifice offered for us was sufficient and accepted by God? We know because God did not let Christ be conquered by death (Rom. 4:25). The once-and-for-all sacrifice had to rise to prove that there was no need for another. In the resurrection, God declared that the blood of Christ availed. The resurrection announced that God was pleased and the blood of Christ was sufficient. "His blood saves because he is risen."[70] His blood availed. His blood still avails.

By the resurrection, God guaranteed that our sins are forgiven (1 Cor. 15:17). Yet, by it He also demonstrated that there is power in the blood of Christ. This power conquers sin in this life and death in the next. Therefore, the Christian never needs to live his or her life below the level of the resurrection because the blood of Christ, as testified by the resurrection of Christ, has secured our lives now and forevermore. In other words, though we look forward to the fullness of resurrection life in the age to come, we should live our lives today in the power and promise of the resurrection.

At one point in John Bunyan's *The Pilgrim's Progress*, Christian and Hopeful are captured by Giant Despair, taken to his Doubting Castle, and thrown into the dungeon. In the dungeon, they are beaten, tempted, and discouraged even to the point of death. Yet, at the last hour, they are able to escape. In fact, they escape early on a Sunday morning. Their release happens not because Giant Despair has a change of heart and suddenly becomes a friend of grace; rather, it is because they realize they have a key. This key unlocks the doors of the dungeon and frees them from Doubting Castle. The key is *promise*:

> Well, on Saturday about midnight they began to pray, and continued in prayer till almost the break of day. Now a little before daylight, good Christian broke out in this passionate speech: "What fool I am to lie in a stinking dungeon when I can freely walk away! I have a key in my bosom called Promise, that will, I am persuaded, open any lock in Doubting Castle." Then said Hopeful, "That is good news, good brother: pull it out of your bosom and try."
>
> Then Christian pulled out the key of Promise and began to try the dungeon door; and as he turned it, the bolt slid back and the door flew open with ease, and Christian and Hopeful both came out.[71]

This key is the promise of resurrection. It is the promise that while Friday is dark, Sunday is coming. It is the promise of God that, in securing the life of Christ, He also will secure the lives of all those who trust in Him. The promise is that He, who vindicated Christ in the resurrection, will vindicate us as well (1 Tim. 3:16; Ps. 35:24). The resurrection avails for us because the blood availed for us.

Let the blood of Christ avail for you. As we have seen, there is power in the blood. The power belongs to Christ. He desires for us to avail ourselves of it. He desires that we live in, through,

119

and by His blood. In other words, we should live as the people we are according to His blood. We are redeemed, restored, forgiven, adopted, and eternally blessed. We live our lives as more than conquerors when we see the blood as our appropriation of all that we are and have in union with Christ.

But how can we do this? How can we appropriate the blood of Christ so as to have it avail for us in our daily lives? We must speak, sing, savor, and seek.

Speak the Words of Faith

"Let the redeemed of the LORD say so" (Ps. 107:2). When given the opportunity to speak of the great salvation we have in Christ, do it! The words of life not only bring life to others, but they strengthen life in us. When we refuse to speak up and declare the work of Christ in dying for our sins, we not only rob others of the joy that could be theirs, but we also weaken our own resolve to live in the power of the blood and the resurrection. Jesus reminded us that "by your words you will be justified, and by your words you will be condemned" (Matt. 12:37). There are no more important words we can speak than the words proclaiming our justification according to the blood of Christ.

Therefore, let both the meditations of your heart and the words of your mouth proclaim salvation, freedom, redemption, and victory through the blood of the Lamb. When you speak faithfully of the promises of God to save and satisfy all those who come to Him in Christ by His blood, Christ says, "Yes!" And we can confidently say, "Amen!" (2 Cor. 1:20).

Sing the Songs of Victory

As you should have observed from the inclusion of so many hymn excerpts in this book, singing is indispensable to the church and the Christian life. As someone has rightly said, "We sing what we believe and we believe what we sing." Faithful songs serve the church by delivering mind-renewing, heart-encouraging, and emotion-stirring theology. The creative treasure of the church has been the bountiful blessing of singing. Christians sing. And we sing best when we sing Jesus. In fact, we are told that in heaven Christ is worshiped through the singing of a "new song." It is a song that exclaims His sacrificial death and His redeeming blood:

> "Worthy are you to take the scroll and to open its seals,
> for you were slain, and by your blood you ransomed
> people for God from every tribe and language and
> people and nation and you made them a kingdom and
> priests to our God, and they shall reign on the earth."
> (Rev. 5:9–10)

As it is sung in heaven, let us sing on earth. Let the songs we sing resound with the sacrificial work of Christ. Every time we sing, we should make sure there are words reminding us of the power of Christ's blood to save, secure, and satisfy.

The church is a singing organism. Our life's song is focused on the blood of Christ. When we gather, we sing of the blood of Jesus. When we are apart, we should keep singing of the blood that avails for us. People sing about that which is most precious to them. There is nothing more precious to the Christian than the blood of Christ. That's why we sing:

> O precious is the flow
> That makes us white as snow.
> No other fount I know.
> Nothing but the blood of Jesus.[72]

Christians sing because we are the only ones who really have something to sing about. Our songs are not simply about the pleasure of singing in the rain or optimistic anticipation that the sun will come out tomorrow. Our songs are based on the sure foundation of the efficacy of the blood of Christ, blood that will never lose its power. As Andrae Crouch taught us:

> The blood that Jesus shed for me,
> Way back on Calvary;
> The blood that gives me strength from day to day,
> It will never lose its power!
> It reaches to the highest mountain,
> It flows to the lowest valley;
> The blood that gives me strength from day to day,
> It will never lose its power![73]

There is strength to be realized not only in believing on the finished work of Christ, but in singing about it as well. Sing it, and see if you do not realize its strength today.

Savor the Favor of God

Remind yourself daily that Christ did not shed His blood for nothing. The most valuable commodity in the universe, namely, the life of Christ, was given for our souls. This should remind us of how valuable God considers our lives to be. He has delighted to call us sons and daughters. Consequently, there is a favor and blessing upon those for whom Christ died. The world may see a pauper, yet God sees a princess. The world may see a shepherd boy, yet God sees a king. We do not have to curry favor with God; Christ has secured our favor through His blood. Savor it. Walk in it. Thank God for it, knowing that you do not deserve it, yet He delights for you to have it. In fact, the more you know you do not deserve it, the more He is pleased for you to experience it (James 4:10).

God's Word says: "What then shall we say to these things? If God is for us, who can be against us? He who did not spare his own Son but gave him up for us all, how will he not also with him graciously give us all things?" (Rom. 8:31–32). About whom does God speak these words? These are words of promise and comfort to those redeemed by the Son. If God has given Christ for us, what higher favor could He bestow on us? Delight in His goodness—and know that there is more to come (1 Cor. 2:9).

Seek a Better City

There is a city whose builder and maker is God (Heb. 11:10). It is a better city. It is a new city. John Bunyan called it "the Celestial City." And it is ours! It is an eternal dwelling for all those who have placed their faith and trust in Christ; for innumerable angels in festal gathering; for the assembly of the firstborn who are enrolled in heaven; for God, the Judge of all; for the spirits of the righteous made perfect; and for Jesus, the Mediator of a new covenant. We can be there because of the sprinkled blood that speaks a better word than the blood of Abel (Heb. 12:22–24). The blood avails for us so that we can take our eyes off the things of this world and set them on Jesus, where He is, and the promise that we will be with Him someday. There is no greater comfort in life and in death than to know that there is a reality beyond the present one, that this life is not all that there is. The blood of Christ assures us of this. His blood gives us a living hope.

Therefore, seek that for which you have been redeemed; eternal in the heavens (2 Cor. 5:1). Seek the city of God. Seek eternity, and you will be sure to get it. And know that it is the blood of Jesus that makes it possible and worthwhile. As the song says:

> *His blood does make the world appear*
> *Less delightful to all my eye.*
> *He sacrificed to draw me near,*
> *To worship Him with all my life.*[74]

"O PRECIOUS BLOOD"

by Tony Carter; arranged by Allan Bynoe
(East Point Music, 2009)

Appendix 2

SONGS
OF THE BLOOD

Here are some hymns that focus especially on the blood of Christ:

- "And Can It Be That I Should Gain" by Charles Wesley, 1738
- "Are You Washed in the Blood?" by Elisha A. Hoffman, 1878
- "Before the Throne of God Above" by Charitie L. Bancroft, 1863
- "But the Blood" by Kirk Franklin (Bridge Building Brentwood-Benson Publishing/Aunt Gertrude Music Publishing, 2011)
- "Come to the Table" by Michael Card (Mole End Music/Word Music Inc., 1984)
- "Jesus Paid It All" by Elvina M. Hall, 1865

- "Let Your Blood Plead for Me" by Isaac Watts (arranged by Jeremy Quillo and Bobby Gilles, Sojourn Music, 2011)
- "Man of Sorrows, What a Name" by Philip Bliss, 1875
- "Nothing But the Blood" by Robert Lowry, 1876
- "O the Blood" by Thomas Miller and Mary Beth Miller (Gateway Create Publishing/Integrity's Praise! Music, 2010)
- "O for a Thousand Tongues to Sing" by Charles Wesley, 1739
- "O Precious Blood" by Anthony Carter (East Point Music, 2008)
- "Redeemed, How I Love to Proclaim It!" by Fanny Crosby, 1882
- "Redeemed, Restored, Forgiven" by Henry W. Baker, 1876
- "The Blood Will Never Lose Its Power" by Andrae Crouch (Manna Music, 1966)
- "There Is a Fountain Filled with Blood" by William Cowper, 1772
- "There Is Power in the Blood" by Lewis E. Jones, 1899
- "Victory in Jesus" by Eugene Bartlett, 1939

Notes

1 From the hymn "Nothing But the Blood" by Robert Lowry, 1876.

2 From the hymn "There Is a Fountain Filled with Blood" by William Cowper, 1771.

3 Richard Phillips, ed., *Precious Blood: The Atoning Work of Christ* (Wheaton, Ill.: Crossway, 2009), 9.

4 Stephen Charnock, *A Discourse on the Cleansing Virtue of Christ's Blood* (Gatineau, QC: Solus Christus, 2011), 10.

5 Alan Stibbs, *His Blood Works: The Meaning of the Word 'Blood' in Scripture* (Rossshire, Scotland: Christian Focus, 2011), 20. According to Stibbs, "The distribution is as follows: Matthew (1), Mark (1), John (4), Acts (1), Pauline epistles (8), Hebrews (6), 1 Peter (2), 1 John (3), Revelation (4)" (note 1, p. 20).

6 From the hymn "There Is a Fountain Filled with Blood."

7 Joel Beeke, in *Precious Blood*, 26.

8 According to Stibbs, "Blood is a visible token of life violently ended; it is a sign of life either given or taken in death" (*His Blood Works*, 80).

9 James Montgomery Boice, *Genesis: An Expositional Commentary, Vol. 1* (Grand Rapids: Baker, 1998), 251. Admittedly, some believe that God's rejection of Cain's sacrifice was due only to Cain's lack of faith and humility in approaching God, and not a consequence of his bloodless offering. However, it can be argued that the difference between God's reaction to Cain's and Abel's sacrifices was not just in the offerers but also in the offerings. Theologian Michael Horton writes: "These offerings were not simply a matter of divine or human whim. It was not as if God had commanded that they bring whatever they felt like on a given day. Nor was it an arbitrary choice on God's part. Even this early in redemptive history, 'without the shedding of blood there is no forgiveness' (Heb. 9:22)." (*In the Face of God: The Dangers and Delights of Spiritual Intimacy* [Dallas: Word, 1996], 8).

10 From the song "Nothing But the Blood" by Matt Redman (Thankyou Music, 2004).

11 From the hymn "Redeemed, How I Love to Proclaim It!" by Fanny Crosby, 1882.

12 From the hymn "O Precious Blood" by Tony Carter; arranged by Allan Bynoe (East Point Music, 2009). See Appendix 1.

13 From the hymn "Victory in Jesus" by Eugene Bartlett, 1939.

14 Herman Hoeksema, *The Triple Knowledge: An Exposition of the Heidelberg Catechism*, Vol. 1 (Grand Rapids: Reformed Free Publishing, 1970), 42.

15 From the hymn "Victory in Jesus."

16 From the hymn "O Precious Blood."

17 J. I. Packer, *Knowing God* (Downers Grove, Ill.: InterVarsity, 1973), 181.

18 William Hendricksen, *Romans*, New Testament Commentary (Grand Rapids: Baker, 1981), 132.

19 Jerry Bridges, *Respectable Sins: Confronting the Sins We Tolerate* (Colorado Springs, Colo.: NavPress, 2007), 121.

20 Shai Linne, "Atonement Q&A" (Lampmode Recordings, 2008).

21 From the hymn "From Whence This Fear and Unbelief" by Augustus Toplady, 1772.

22 From the hymn "Man of Sorrows! What a Name" by Philip P. Bliss, 1875.

23 Attributed to an Ohio newspaper, *The Huron Reflector*, Nov. 23, 1841.

24 R. C. Sproul, *Essential Truths of the Christian Faith* (Wheaton, Ill.: Tyndale House, 1992), 189.

25 Westminster Shorter Catechism, Question 14.

26 From the song "Let Your Blood Plead for Me" by Isaac Watts, Jeremy Quillo, and Bobby Gilles (Sojourn Music, 2011).

27 From the hymn "The Love of God" by Frederick M. Lehman, 1917.

28 From the song "How Deep the Father's Love for Us" by Stuart Townend (Kingsway Thankyou Music, 1995).

29 From the hymn "There Is a Fountain Filled with Blood."

30 Wayne Grudem, *Systematic Theology* (Grand Rapids: Zondervan, 1994), 673.

31 From the hymn "How Sweet and Awful Is the Place" by Isaac Watts, 1707.

32 Sinclair Ferguson, *Know Your Christian Life: A Theological Introduction* (Downers Grove, Ill.: InterVarsity, 1981), 103.

33 Paul Jewett, *Election and Predestination* (Grand Rapids: Eerdmans, 1985), 1.

34   From the song "There Is a Redeemer" by Tom Fettke and Keith Green (Universal Music Publishing Group).

35   From the hymn "Come, Thou Fount of Every Blessing" by Robert Robinson, 1758.

36   John R. W. Stott, *The Message of Ephesians* (Downers Grove, Ill.: InterVarsity, 1979), 96.

37   William Hendricksen, *Galatians, Ephesians, Philippians, Colossians, and Philemon* (Grand Rapids: Baker, 1996), 129.

38   From the song "Back on the Block" by Quincy Jones (Warner Bros., 1989).

39   From the hymn "Come, Thou Fount of Every Blessing."

40   Stott, *The Message of Ephesians*, 97.

41   From the hymn "Lead Me to Calvary" by Jennie E. Hussey, 1921.

42   From the hymn "Redeemed, Restored, Forgiven" by Henry W. Baker, 1876.

43   Eugene Peterson, *A Long Obedience in the Same Direction: Discipleship in an Instant Society* (Downers Grove, Ill.: InterVarsity, 1980), 52.

44   Walter Brueggeman, *Peace* (St. Louis: Chalice Press, 2001), 16. Brueggeman goes on to say, "Creation in Genesis and by Jesus (see Colossians 1:17) is the establishment of shalom in a universe that apart from God's rule is disordered, unproductive, and unfulfilling."

45   Wilhelmus à Brakel, *The Christian's Reasonable Service*, Vol. 2 (Grand Rapids: Reformation Heritage Books, 440.

46   Stibbs, *His Blood Works*, 61.

47   From the hymn "Redeemed, Restored, Forgiven."

48   Charles Spurgeon, *Morning and Evening* (Peabody, Mass.: Hendrickson, 1991), 209.

49   From the hymn "Are You Washed in the Blood?" by Elisha A. Hoffman, 1878.

50   From the hymn "Are You Washed in the Blood?"

51   From the hymn "There Is a Fountain Filled with Blood."

52   R. C. Sproul, *The Holiness of God*, 2nd ed. (Wheaton, Ill.: Tyndale House, 1998), 26.

53   Charnock, *A Discourse on the Cleansing Virtue of Christ's Blood*, 19.

54   J. I. Packer, *18 Words: The Most Important Words You Will Ever Know* (Ross-shire, Scotland: Christian Focus, 2007), 169.

55   John Bunyan, *The Pilgrim's Progress* (Uhrichsville, Ohio: Barbour Publishing, 1988), 61.

56 From the hymn "Before the Throne of God Above" by Charitie L. Bancroft, 1863.

57 From the hymn "And Can It Be That I Should Gain" by Charles Wesley, 1738.

58 Grudem, *Systematic Theology*, 670.

59 Thomas Goodwin, quoted in *A Puritan Golden Treasury*, compiled by I. D. E. Thomas (Edinburgh: Banner of Truth, 1997), 83.

60 Charles Spurgeon, "Defense of Calvinism," in *The Five Points of Calvinism*, 2nd edition, by David N. Steele, Curtis C. Thomas, and S. Lance Quinn (Phillipsburg, N.J.: P&R Publishing, 2004), 173.

61 From the hymn "And Can it Be That I Should Gain."

62 From the hymn "Jesus Paid It All" by Elvina M. Hall, 1865.

63 From the hymn "Why Should I Fear?" by William Williams.

64 Stibbs, *His Blood Works*, 44.

65 From the hymn "Jesus Paid It All."

66 Mrs. Howard Taylor, *Borden of Yale* (Minneapolis: Bethany House, 1988), 162.

67 From the hymn "There Is Power in the Blood" by Lewis E. Jones, 1899.

68 Spurgeon, *Morning and Evening*, 214.

69 From the hymn "O for a Thousand Tongues to Sing" by Charles Wesley, 1739.

70 Sam Allberry, *Lifted: Experiencing the Resurrection Life* (Phillipsburg, N.J.: P&R Publishing, 2012), 35.

71 John Bunyan, *The New Pilgrim's Progress*, updated text by Judith E. Markham and notes by Warren W. Wiersbe (Grand Rapids: Discovery House, 1989), 160.

72 From the hymn "Nothing But the Blood."

73 From the song "The Blood Will Never Lose Its Power" by Andrae Crouch (Manna Music, 1966).

74 From the hymn "O Precious Blood."

Scripture Index

About the Author

Anthony J. Carter serves as the lead pastor of East Point Church in the Atlanta, Ga., area.

He holds a bachelor's degree from Atlanta Christian College and a master's degree in biblical studies from Reformed Theological Seminary in Orlando, Fla. He is the author of *On Being Black and Reformed: A New Perspective on the African-American Christian Experience*, and the editor of *Glory Road: The Journeys of Ten African-Americans into Reformed Christianity* and *Experiencing the Truth: Bringing the Reformation to the African-American Church*.

Anthony and his wife, Adriane, make their home in East Point, Ga. They have five children.